MILLET BUSINESS IDEAS

Empowering Millet Startups

TAPAS CHANDRA ROY

MILLET BUSINESS IDEAS

Empowering Millet Startups

Copyright © Tapas Chandra Roy 2022

All rights reserved. This book or any portion thereof may not be reproduced or used in any manner whatsoever without the express written permission of the author except for the use of brief quotations in a book review.

First Published by: Tapas Chandra Roy in 2022

Edition: 1

Publisher's Address: Mahaveer Lane, Pujariput, Koraput, Odisha – 764020

Printed in India

ISBN: 9798361501960

All Rights Reserved.

www.milletadvisor.com

tapas@milletadvisor.com

I dedicate this book to my parents, my loving and caring wife Shradha, my little daughter Dona and everyone who has touched my life in some way or the other and made it so special.

Foreword

Welcome to the *millet movement* being led globally by India. Many millets originate from India and India has the largest number of different types of millets grown compared to any country in the world and the widest range of millet products in the world.

Key players responsible for the turnaround in the millet industry include food processing entrepreneurs. They are true pioneers and social entrepreneurs who have discovered the amazing health and environmental benefits of millets and dedicated their efforts to reviving this amazing ancient grain.

These millet pioneers have painstakingly designed products, educated the markets, run cooking demonstrations and nutrition information sessions, and spread the word far and wide, changing the image of millets to modern delicious food. Many have personally had their own health concerns turned around by changing their diets to be millet-based and so are living advocates of the benefits of millets.

This book, "MILLET BUSINESS IDEAS - Empowering Millet Start-ups" represents a massive effort to collate valuable information on millets that can highly benefit start-ups and existing entrepreneurs to advance the industry to the next level.

As the industry matures, it is critical to ensure that millets remain whole grain when eaten to help reverse increasing diabetes, obesity, and heart diseases. It is also important to remember that if you add fats/sugar/salt/synthetic additives you can make anything tasty. Let's stay true to the super nutritional and health benefits of millets! The millet entrepreneurs have proven millet dishes can be delicious without ultra-processing or unhealthy additives.

This is also the time to connect farmers with processors, create streamlined supply chains, and ensure that farmers benefit from

www.ingramcontent.com/pod-product-compliance
Lightning Source LLC
LaVergne TN
LVHW010121170826
845678LV00012B/2525
9798223503972

an emerging industry fairly. Seed systems that engage farmers and protect the traditional varieties should also be part of the developments.

Reaching the masses is also important which will require bringing millets back as a staple. This is a key way we can have a big impact on the health of people and the planet and benefit the farmers. Special attention needs to be focused on millet rice to achieve this, supported by level playing fields for policy and investments, and developing the global markets and supply chains.

A huge congratulations to Tapas Chandra Roy for his endless efforts to share knowledge on millets and for compiling such excellent helpful information in this publication! Let's all keep the *millet movement* progressing positively for the benefit of consumers, the planet, and farmers.

Joanna Kane-Potaka

Contents

Foreword
Acknowledgement
Preface

Part I: Understanding Millets

1. What are Millets and their types 01
2. Nutritional Value of each millet.............................15
3. Health Benefits of Millets with scientific study...........23
4. Myths and Beliefs about millets 29

Part II: Current Trends of Millets

1. Millet Value Chain Analysis 33
2. Consumption trends in current and future context ... 41
3. Government Initiatives in promoting Millets 45

Part III: Millet Business Ideas with success stories

1. Millet Value Addition 55
2. Millet milk- an alternative to Dairy milk 63
3. Millet-based Hotel Industry and Millet Cloud Kitchen...65
4. Millet Cutlery – improving hygiene and saving the earth from waste and pollution 69
5. Bird Feed Industry – Meeting the nutritional needs of the pet birds 71
6. Establishing a Primary Processing Unit 73
7. Millet Bakery Unit 81
8. Millet Baby Food Products 87
9. Millet Export Business – Taking Indian Millets to the International Markets 93
10. Millet Social Entrepreneurship – Empowering Women...103
11. Organic and Natural Millets 109

12. Millet Recipes Ideas – Teaching how to cook millets perfectly 111
13. Millet Beverages Industry - Booming in Future 115

Part IV: Growing Millet Business Digitally

1. Millet Brand Building 121

Part V: Support to start Millet Startups

1. Institutional Support in India 131
2. State and Central Government Schemes for Millet Startups 135
3. Central Government and State Millet Missions 137

Part VI: Points to consider before beginning Millet Start-ups

1. Challenges in Millets and how to overcome 151
2. Understanding end users' needs and building innovative products 155

References 159

About Author *163*

Acknowledgements

‘‘‘’ Success is the progressive realization of a worthy idea’’’’.

- Earl Nightingale,

I take this opportunity to express my sincere gratitude to the Almighty for giving me enough strength in every walk of my life and providing a solid foundation to write this book. Every single day is new learning for me. I look back and see I have undergone a lot of changes during this time. By treasuring the experiences gained, I have made myself flexible and adaptable.

I consider myself fortunate enough to be in the right place with the right people. I take this opportunity to express my deep sense of gratitude and heartfelt thanks to the esteemed organization, the Indian Institute of Millets Research, Hyderabad. I thank Dr.Vilas Tonapi, Ex-Director, IIMR, Dr.Dayakar Rao, Principal Scientist, and Dr.Sangappa for guiding and inspiring me to take forward my journey with millets.
Special thanks to Joanna Kane-Potaka and Raj Bhandari for their continuous support and inspiration to work in the millet space.

I would like to thank Dr. Arabinda Kumar Padhee, Principal Secretary, Department of Agriculture and Farmers' Empowerment, Govt. of Odisha, and Dr. Prem Chand Chaudhary, Director, Directorate of Agriculture and Food Production, Odisha, for providing me with enough opportunities to learn more about millets and to implement Odisha Millet Mission at the ground level.

I extend my thanks to Sweta Samota, an Amazon Bestselling Author who helped and supported me from the book's conception to launching, writing, editing, and publishing. Without her, this book would only be a dream.

Special thanks to Siddharth Rajsekar, India's leading digital coach, for making me understand all the digital platforms and connecting with the people in India. His teaching helped me write one of the chapters on millet brand building.

Special thanks to everyone who allowed me to share their stories in this book. Particular thanks to Raja Shekar Reddy, Meghana Narayan, Shauravi Malik, Prashant Parameswaran, Krishnaa Kantthawala, Vishala Reddy Vuyyala, Saravanan, Raju Bhupati, Sweta Khandelwal, Chittem Sudheer, Bharat Reddy, Narayan Peesapathy, Shaila Gurudutt, Lakshmi Bheemachar, Natasha Gandhi, Shalini Santhosh, Murugan S, Sucheta Bhandare, Shalini Rajani and Santosh Kumar Khemundu.

Thanks to the encouragement, support, and inspiration from my higher authority, colleagues, and department staff.

Without the selfless love, support, and blessings of my loving parents, family, friends, and well-wishers, my efforts would not be fruitful. Thank you so much to all.

Thank you to everyone who follows me on Youtube, LinkedIn, Facebook, Twitter, and Instagram and subscribers to my newsletters. Yours every like, comment, and share gives me inspiration and encouragement.

Lastly, I convey my sincere thanks to you - all the readers of this book. Because of you, the thought came to me, and I took the opportunity to bring forth my learnings, knowledge, and experiences in the millet field for nine years. I hope you will imbibe my ideas and thoughts in your millet startup journey.

Preface

Welcome to the Millet Startup Journey

This book cover depicts something special. The book cover shows its importance taking into account the surrounding light. In this, two colors are chosen, i.e., black and white.
In the lighter part, we can visualize the "Millet Business," but the "ideas" were in the complete dark. When the light was on, we could see the "IDEAS." The IDEAS turned white color showing its prominence.

To start any journey, you must have a particular goal or idea. If a person is working on a predetermined goal or idea and knows where he/she is going, then the person is a success. Otherwise, the person is a failure. This book has tried to bring out the ideas and opportunities in the millet sector to you. It also covers successful stories of the millet entrepreneurs who have accomplished specific goals in their millet startup journey. I have also shared the experiences I have gained since nine years working with millet. The issues and the problems faced by the new millet entrepreneurs pushed me to write this book for you.
This book will be useful for those who have started their millet startup journey before and want to do better with the next one.

Indeed, this book on "" Millet Business Ideas"" will empower the millet startups as it is the need of the hour in our country. 2023 will be celebrated as the International year of millets.
This book will indirectly help the small and marginal millet farmers of our country as they are the first stakeholders in the millet value chain. The millet startups will build the forward linkage and connect farmers with the consumers delivering the right product that will help in building a healthy nation.

Let's get a brief overview of the chapters in this book:

Chapter 1 discusses the basic understanding of the millets. This chapter highlights the millets and their types, the Nutritional value of all nine types of millets grown in India along with the health benefits.

Chapter 2 describes the current trends of millets, giving the complete millet value chain analysis covering millet production, processing, and value addition. It also emphasizes the millet consumption trends both in current and future contexts. In addition, it briefly describes the government initiatives in promoting millet in India and abroad.

Chapter 3 walks the reader through all the millet business opportunities for entrepreneurs with stories of the successful millet entrepreneurs in the field of millet processing, millet bakery industry, millet value addition, millet milk, millet baby foods, millet hotel and cloud kitchen, millet export from India, teaching how to cook millets, millet social entrepreneurship, millet cutlery, bird feed industry, organic and natural millets and millet beverages industry.

Chapter 4 introduces the digital world and explores various online platforms and tools to grow the millet business digitally and the steps and procedures for millet brand building. It covers the marketing tools required for brand building covering website user expertise, SEO and content promotion, social media promotion, email promotion, paid advertising, and analytics.

Chapter 5 describes the institutional support in India given to start Millet Startups and briefly explains the schemes available for Millet Startups, and covers the Central Government Schemes and State Millet Missions of Andhra Pradesh, Chhattisgarh, Karnataka, Maharashtra, Odisha, and Telangana.

Chapter 6 emphasizes the points to consider before starting a millet startup. Explore the challenges faced in the millet sector and understand the end user's needs and build innovative millet products.

This book will act as the guidebook for all the budding entrepreneurs willing to take a step in building their millet startups. It will also benefit scientists, students, researchers, policymakers, FPOs, Self-help groups, and institutions working in the development sectors.

PART- I

UNDERSTANDING MILLETS

One

MILLETS AND TYPES OF MILLETS IN INDIA

What are millets? Ever wondered what is so special about millets? Why are they called Climate Smart Crops?

Millets are a group of small-seeded cereal food crops belonging to the Poaceae family. It has been utilized as food, feed, and fodder from immemorial days. Millets are among the ancient food grains of India primarily grown on marginal land in dry areas.

Unlike cereals, Millets are adapted to a wide range of ecological conditions demanding less water and inputs, and fit well even in infertile soil, taking a short period to grow to make them climate resilient. When we say resilient crops, it means tolerant against extreme climatic conditions including drought and flood.

As you know, we are in the era of climate change and to address it, Millets are the ideal crop.

The recent change in climate has led to a decrease in the yield of major staple cereals and this phenomenon has paved the path for the introduction of millet into the agriculture production system.

That's not the only reason why millets are so wonderful. The short life cycle of 60-90 days facilitates escaping the stress, ensuring food for the marginal farmers who primarily depend on farming. There are millets in the hilly areas which mature early. Sometimes these millets become the first crop to be harvested and consumed as food while waiting for other crops to mature.

Millet requires 350-450 mm of rain to grow and gives a better yield, whereas rice requires 1200 mm of rainfall; otherwise, it falls into the trap of drought. These fulfilling qualities of millets make them widely accepted by farmers.

Millets are widely consumed in Asia and Africa, covering 59 million people. However, the preference for a single cereal-based diet has slowly made millet food disappear from the plate; now, it's time to revive millets back because they are the only crop that will address critical issues in the future like food, feed, malnutrition, health, and climate change.

The world production of millets is 89.17 million metric tonnes in an area of 74 million ha, whereas the position of India in the global market is the leader in the production of millets with a share of 41%. India produces about 16 million metric tonnes of millet with a yield of 1247kg per ha. It is grown in about 12.45 million ha. Pearl Millet (Bajra) takes the share of 50% of the country's area under millets. India is the top producer of Little Millet, Kodo Millet, Finger Millet, Barnyard Millet, and Pearl Millet, covering an area of 8.87 million ha.

As per the final estimates of DES, Government of India, 2021-22, Sorghum is grown in an area of 4.83 million ha. with an average yield of 989 kg per ha. It is seen that the production and productivity of Sorghum are better during the Rabi season.

Millets are well connected to the food system and culture, and it is the source of livelihood for small and marginal farmers. Millets are referred to as superfoods. These millet grains have high nutritional features and health benefits. Millet production can be seen as an approach to sustainable agriculture and a healthy world. Millet farming results in preserving and conserving biodiversity.

It must definitely be coming into your mind that millets have so much goodness in terms of sustainable farming, environment-friendly, and nutrition, but what has happened is that we started talking about millets in the last decade only.

There are many reasons but let me give you some important ones.

- Neglected research and development.
- Underexplored nutrition in millets.
- Devoted the unfertile marginal and unproductive lands for millets.
- Supporting policies of the Government were missing in mainstreaming millets.

But now the power of millets is utilized adequately by giving more importance. This has resulted in an increase in production and productivity even though the area under production of millets has drastically reduced.

With the rise in population and declining food grain production, the Government of India launched the "Green Revolution" program in 1965. This program gave more focus on rice and wheat and subsequently, the research and development and policy shifted its focus from the wonder crop millets.

An intensive monocropping system in rice and wheat, assistance in inputs like seeds and fertilizers, and an assured Government procurement system led to the reduction of area under millets.
Slowly the millet started vanishing from the plates and came under the category of "Forgotten Grains".

The time has again come back to brainstorm and find solutions. It is time for farmers, scientists, and policymakers to search for sustainable alternative crops so that they can address the increasingly erratic climatic conditions, depleting natural resources, health, and nutrition.
This can only happen through continuous policy support like incentivizing millet farmers, establishing decentralized Millet processing units at the ground level, and bringing more awareness among the consumers so that the supply and demand go alongside.

India is the highest producer of millets in the globe and the 5th largest exporter of millets. Millet exports are increasing exponentially as the demand for millet is increasing at a fast rate. Millets are also addressing the need for fuel and feeds. It has the potential to produce biofuel.

As the demand for millet is increasing, it is creating more business opportunities for entrepreneurs. The Millet Market size was over USD 9 billion in 2018 and will witness more than 4.5% CAGR during the forecast time span (2018-2025) and the value projected is more than USD 12 billion. So, it is the right time to grab the opportunities in the millet business sector. Many entrepreneurs have already taken a step and have entered into this segment and are doing good business.

TYPES OF MILLETS:

This chapter will bring the 9 types of millets grown in India. You can find millet-growing areas in every state in India. There is a spatial distribution of millets and it mainly depends upon the rainfall and the growing habitat. If you consider the low-lying areas, where there is stagnant water just after the rain, the millets do not find their place in that situation. But the sloppy and hilly regions providing a natural ecosystem are favorable to growing millets.

Millets are categorized depending on the area and also on the size of the grains. In terms of area, it is divided into major and minor millets. The major millets are Sorghum, Pearl Millet, and Finger Millet which are grown in 90-95% of the total cropping area under millets. The rest millets come under minor millets. Little Millet, Foxtail Millet, Barnyard Millet, Kodo Millet, Proso Millet, and Browntop Millet come under minor millets.

Another category, in which millets are categorized, is the presence and absence of the husk layer. Sorghum, Pearl Millet, and Finger Millets come under naked grains and the rest millets are husked grains. The husked grains require processing to remove the husk for human consumption.

Let us briefly understand the types of millets. Knowing them completely will help us better promote them and bring awareness among the people.

1. Pearl Millet:

Pearl Millet (Pennisetum glaucum) is the most widely grown millet in the world.

The height of the Pearl millet plant ranges from 0.5 to 4 meters. It has giant kernels of all varieties except Sorghum. It is an oval grain of 3-4 mm. Its color varies from white, pale yellow, gray, and slate blue. The weight of 1000 seeds is around 2.5 to 14 g with a mean of 8 grams.

It has been grown since prehistoric times in the Indian subcontinent and African countries. Around 4500 BC the Pearl Millet was domesticated in northern-central Sahelian Africa. Basically, Pearl Millet originated in Western Africa.

It has been reported that about 90 million people depend upon it for food and to sustain a livelihood. It is preferably grown in drier areas, where there is low rainfall. It can tolerate drought, low fertility, and high temperature.

In India, Rajasthan is the largest producer of Pearl Millet. It can be grown in different types of soil but care is to be taken not to grow in waterlogged areas. It is well suited for crop rotation and double cropping.

Photo: *A trial plot in Koraput, Odisha.*

2. Sorghum:

Sorghum (Sorghum bicolor) originated in northern-eastern Africa. About 5000-8000 years ago, it was domesticated. The Sorghum grain color, shape, and size vary according to the variety. The pericarp colors are white, red, and yellow. The seed size varies from 4-6 mm. The maturity of the grains is detected by the presence of dark spots on the grains.

It is a warm-season crop intolerant to low temperatures and a climate-compliant crop. It ranks fifth in the cereals produced worldwide and fourth in India. Being a C4 plant, it efficiently uses solar energy and water to produce biomass and food.

The C4 plant uses a specific photosynthesis mechanism (C4 photosynthesis) in order to avoid photorespiration. As food, it is the principal source of protein, vitamins, energy, and minerals for millions of people in semi-arid regions.

We call "Sorghum a wonder grain" due to its versatility and space in every sector like Food, Feed, and Fuel.

The Sorghum grain color, shape, and size vary according to the variety. The pericarp colors are white, red, and yellow. The seed size varies from 4-6 mm. The maturity of the grains is detected by the presence of dark spots on the grains.

3. Finger Millet:

Finger Millet (Eleusine coracana), commonly known as Ragi.

The seed type of Finger Millet is Utricle and the shape of the grain is globose. The testa of the grain is pigmented with thick five-cell layers. The endosperm is the largest component of the kernel. The aleurone layer is single and it lies just below the seed coat and testa. Finger Millet grains are 1-2 mm in diameter with the color varying from brown to dark brown. 1000 kernel weight is 2.3 gms.

It is grown for cereal and fodder purposes under various agro-climatic conditions in India. It is the primary food of the rural and tribal populations of Southern India and East and Central Africa. It is seen to have originated in the hills of western Tanzania or Ethiopian highlands. There are wide ranges of landraces and each of them has unique properties in terms of taste and nutrition. Due to the ease of processing and value addition, it is widely accepted as food in Southern and Eastern Africa and South Asia.

The major Finger Millet growing states are Karnataka, Uttarakhand, Andhra Pradesh, Odisha, Tamil Nadu, Jharkhand, and Maharashtra.

Finger Millet Panicles (Variety: GPU-66)

4. Foxtail Millet:

Foxtail Millet (Setaria italica) is the oldest cultivated millet in the world. The seed type of Foxtail Millet is Caryopsis. The grains are about 2-3 mm in length and the color of the glumes can be red, white, black, white, or yellow.

It was domesticated more than 8000 years ago in China. It is the staple cereal in the arid and semi-arid regions and contributes to the development of Chinese civilization. It is cultivated in about 23 countries in Asia, Africa, and America. Being a short-duration crop, it attains growth quickly and helps in escaping from the drought. It can be grown in a wide range of elevations, soil, and temperatures but need to ensure and protect from water logging.

For human consumption, the outer husk is to be removed by processing. It is also used for chicken and cage birds and for the fodder of livestock.

Foxtail Millet Panicle - Indigenous Variety

5. Little Millet:

Little Millet (Panicum sumatrense) is a short-duration and fast-growing cereal crop that can withstand both drought and waterlog conditions. It is similar to Proso Millet in appearance but in general, is smaller than it. As the name implies, it is the smallest among all millets. The size of the grain is 2-3 mm in length and the shape varies from elliptical to oval shape. The color ranges from gray to straw white.

It is domesticated in the Eastern ghats of India and its origin is not well documented. It is found in large proportions in the diet of the tribal people in the states of India, Myanmar, and Sri Lanka. In India, it is confined to the tribal areas of Odisha, Madhya Pradesh, Chhattisgarh, and Andhra Pradesh. It does not require much care and some tribals called it a lazy crop because the farmers have to visit the field only twice, once for sowing and then for harvesting.

Little Millet Panicle - Indigenous Variety

6. Barnyard Millet:

Barnyard Millet (Echinochloa frumentacea) grain color varies from straw white, gray, and little gray to dull white. The size of the grain is about 3 mm in length. The grain is concave to oval in shape.

Barnyard Millet is widely cultivated as minor cereals for food and fodder in India, Europe, Australia, Korea North America, and the semi-arid tropics of Africa. In India, Barnyard Millet is mainly grown in Andhra Pradesh, Uttarakhand, Uttar Pradesh, Karnataka, Tamil Nadu, Bihar, Gujarat, Chhattisgarh, and Madhya Pradesh. There is not much information on the origin of Barnyard Millet.

Barnyard Millet is the fastest growing of all millets as there are some varieties that are ready to harvest in just six weeks.

7. Proso Millet:

Proso Millet (Panicum miliaceum) grains are spherical to oval in shape. Its length and diameter are about 3mm and 2mm respectively. The color of the grain varies from white cream, golden yellow, brown, and straw white. There are prominent longitudinal lines on the grain by which we can easily differentiate from others. The seed type is Utricle.

Proso Millet offers better prospects for intensive farming. It even yields reasonable harvests in extreme soil and climatic conditions. It is found to be cultivated in the drier regions of Africa, Asia, Europe, Australia, and North America. It is utilized as human food after processing and the unhusked grains are used as bird feed.

8. Kodo Millet:

Kodo Millet (Paspalum scrobiculatum) originated in tropical Africa. The color of the grain may vary from light red to dark brown in color. Kodo Millet grains are elliptical to oval in shape. The size of the grain is about 3-4 mm in length. It is mainly grown in Chhattisgarh, Madhya Pradesh, Karnataka, Tamil Nadu, Telangana, Andhra Pradesh, Bihar, Maharashtra, and Odisha.

Around 3000 years ago it was domesticated in India. Kodo Millet has the ability to grow in the poorest soil. Generally, it is a long-duration crop and it requires 100-140 days to mature. It is an annual tufted grass that grows to 90 cm in height. Due to the presence of multiple seed coats, it becomes very difficult to remove the husk. It is known by multiple names like Indian Crow grass, Ditch millet, Rice grass, and Native Paspalum. It is often seen in paddy fields and considered a weed.

Kodo Millet in the trial plot of IIMR, Hyderabad

9. Browntop Millet:

Browntop Millet (Urochloa ramosa) grains are ellipsoid in shape and tan-white in color. The size of the grains varies from 4-5 mm in length.

Browntop Millet is a native to India and it is grown in limited areas of Andhra Pradesh and Karnataka. In the United States, it is grown in the South-East for hay, pasture and bird feeds. It is found to be grown in plantation areas. It is known as Korale in Kannada. This crop is more popular in the Chitradurga, Tumakuru, and Chikkaballapura districts of Karnataka state.

It can be planted from mid-April until mid-August in most locations. Late sowing results in lower yield.

Two

NUTRITIONAL VALUE OF MILLETS

India is food self-sufficient and moving towards becoming a food surplus country. The vision of the policymakers is shifting from food security to Nutritional security. The government of India as well as some State governments has made significant changes in reviving back the millet.

One of the milestones in the growth of millet in India is that it was renamed from Coarse Cereals to Nutri-Cereals through an official Gazette Notification in 2018 and the year was declared the National Year of Millets.

NOTIFICATION New Delhi, the 10th April 2018 F.No.4-4/2017-NFSM (E) -

Whereas, millets hold great potential in contributing substantially to food and nutritional security of the country and thus they are not only a powerhouse of nutrients but also are climate resilient crops and possess unique nutritional characteristics; And whereas, recent research findings also show that millets contain anti-diabetic properties and millet-based food have a low GI and reduce the postprandial blood glucose level and glycosylated hemoglobin; And whereas, a Committee constituted by the Central Government for examination of inclusion of millets in the Public Distribution System (PDS) for improving nutritional support has recommended for inclusion of millets in PDS across the country and the same has been accepted by the Central Government.

Now, therefore, the Central Government hereby declares millets comprising Sorghum (Jowar), Pearl Millet (Bajra), Finger Millet (Ragi/Mandua), Minor Millets i.e. Foxtail Millet (Kangani/Kakun), Proso Millet (Cheena), Kodo Millet (Kodo), Barnyard Millet (Sawa/Jhangora), Little Millet (Kutki) and two Pseudo Millets [Black-wheat (Kuttu) and Amaranthus (Chaulai) which have high nutritive value as "Nutri-Cereals" for production, consumption and trade point of view.

Millets have the power to address nutritional security in India. Millets are the staples of millions of people in the world. They are nutritionally comparable to major crops like wheat and rice. They serve as a good source of micronutrients, proteins, and phytochemicals.

Knowing the nutritional value of each millet is very important to start a business around this domain. Millet's nutritional value changes depending on the extent of processing. Complete removal of the bran layer of the millet affects its nutrient content. The Bran of the millet is a rich source of dietary fiber.
The use of millet as a whole grain makes the essential nutrients such as minerals, dietary fiber, phenolics, and vitamins concentrated in the outer layer of the grain and offers nutritional benefits.

We know that there are 9 types of millets grown in India. But under each type of millet, there are many varieties and landraces. Each variety possesses different and unique nutritional properties. So, nutritional profiling of each variety is important when you start your startup because going deep will give extra mileage to reach the end consumers.

The research and scientific studies have given us enough evidence of the nutritional value of millet. Let us see the unique nutritional value of each millet.

1. Finger Millet:

Finger Millets are highly nutritious and known to contain the highest amount of Calcium (364 mg/100g) and are rich in iron, zinc, dietary fiber, and essential amino acids.

Nutrients	**Content in %**
Protein	5-8 %
Carbohydrates	65-75 %
Dietary Fiber	15-20 %
Minerals	2.5 - 3.5 %

Its proteins are unique due to the content of sulfur-rich amino acids. The essential amino acids of Finger Millet are arginine, lysine, methionine, and lecithin. The total phospholipid present in Finger Millet is 0.36%. There were five phospholipids of which three were lecithins and the rest two were cephalins.

The soaking and germination of millet is the most popular practice adopted by Indian households. A study was conducted for their influence on the antioxidant profile, anti-nutrient factors, and biochemical properties. In this, it was found that there was the highest reduction of tannins in Finger Millet (2.07 mg/g). With 24 hours of soaking and 24 hours of germination of Finger Millet, the saponin content was found to be 34.86 mg/g.
A study also showed that by soaking and germination of Finger Millet the bioavailability of Calcium increases in the body.

So, by following soaking and germination practices, nutritionally enriched millet products can be produced.

2. Pearl Millet:

Nutrients	Content per 100 g
Iron	6.42 mg
Zinc	2.76 mg
Dietary Fiber	11.4 g
Fat	5.43 g

Pearl Millet also contains a high proportion of proteins (12-16%) as well as lipids (4-6%). ICRISAT and Mahatma Phule Krishi Vidyapeeth jointly developed a high iron content variety of Pearl Millet under the biofortification program. The variety is named "Dhanashakti" and was released in 2012 in Maharashtra.

Dhanashakti has iron of 71 mg/kg and 40mg/kg of zinc. ICRISAT has also developed another Pearl Millet variety (ICMH120) named Shakti1201. This variety contains 75mg/kg iron and 40 mg/kg Zinc. It is almost the same in the iron and zinc content as Dhanashakti but the performance of Shakti1201 is 30% higher.

When Pearl Millet is used for making any product, there is a need to mention the specific cultivars so that the nutritional value of the product catches the attention of the end consumers.

3. Sorghum:

According to the report of the National Institute for Nutrition, Hyderabad every 100 grams of Sorghum grains contains nutrients as per the table below:

Nutrients	Content per 100 gm
Carbohydrates	67.7 g
Protein	9.9 g
Fats	1.73 g
Dietary Fiber	10.2 g
Magnesium	133 mg
Folic acid	39.4 µg
Calcium	27.6 mg
Phosphorous	274 mg
Zinc	1.9 mg
Thiamine	0.35 mg
Riboflavin	0.14 mg
Niacin	2.1 mg

Sorghum is known to be rich in phenolic compounds that act as antioxidants.

4. Little Millet:

Little millet is an excellent source of protein (10.13 g), dietary fiber (7.72 g), carbohydrates (65.55 g), iron(1.26 mg), phosphorus (130 mg/g) and magnesium (91.41 mg) per 100 g. Little Millet also contains amino acids in balanced proportions. It is rich in methionine, lysine, and cysteine.

As Little millet is rich in methionine and cysteine and these amino acids are deficient in pulses, a judicious combination of Little millet and pulses would provide high-quality protein.

5. Foxtail Millet:

Foxtail Millet is rich in protein (12.3 g), crude fiber (8g), fat (4.3 g), Carbohydrates (60.9 g), and micronutrients like iron (2.8 g), zinc (2.4 g), magnesium (81 mg) and potassium (250 mg) per 100 g. It also contains amylose (17.5%), amylopectin (82.5%), calcium (31 mg), and phosphorus (290 mg). Foxtail Millet contains balanced amino acids like arginine, histidine, lysine, tryptophan, phenylalanine, tyrosine, methionine, cystine, leucine, isoleucine, and valine.

Foxtail millet also contains a good profile of vitamins like thiamine (0.59 mg), niacin (3.2 mg), riboflavin (0.11 mg), folic acid (15 mg), Vitamin A (32 mg), Vitamin B5(0.82 mg) and Vitamin E (31 mg).

6. Barnyard Millet:

Barnyard millet is a tremendous source of protein, dietary fiber, calcium, phosphorus, magnesium, zinc, iron, thiamine, riboflavin, niacin, and folic acid. The presence of phytochemicals and phenolic compounds enriches its antioxidant activity and makes it a superior grain.

When Barnyard Millet is compared by taking polished and unpolished grains the nutritional value changes. This shows that the whole grain or the unpolished barnyard millet offers a better range of nutrients and phytochemicals than polished grains.

Quantitative Analysis of Nutrients present in Barnyard Millet (100 g)

Sl. No.	Nutrients	Polished (mean)	Unpolished(mean)
1	Carbohydrates (gm)	65.79 ± 0.02	68.8 ± 0.11
2	Protein (gm)	6.8 ± 0.08	10.4 ± 0.02
3	Dietary fiber (gm)	8.5 ± 1.3	14.2 ± 0.28

4	Crude Fiber (gm)	4.5 ± 0.35	11.2 ± 0.08
5	Calcium (mg)	24.8 ± 0.38	35 ± 0.10
6	Iron (mg)	6.2 ± 0.02	7.1 ± 0.11
7	Thiamine (mg)	0.37 ± 0.01	0.45 ± 0.04
8	Niacin (mg)	4.05 ± 0.02	4.08 ± 0.01
9	Biotin (µg)	20 ± 0.20	22 ± 0.16
10	Folate (µg)	69 ± 0.30	78 ± 0.01

7. Kodo Millet

Kodo Millet is rich in vitamins, minerals, and phytochemicals. It is also rich in essential amino acids like lysine, threonine, valine, and sulfur-containing amino acids and the ratio of leucine to isoleucine is about 2.0 (Ravindram, 1992, Antony et al, 1996). Kodo Millet is rich in vitamin B3, Vitamin B6 as well as minerals such as calcium (15.27 g), magnesium (122 mg), phosphorus (101 mg), and zinc (1.65 mg) per 100g.

It contains dietary fiber of 6.39 g and provides 331 KCal energy per 100 gm of grain. According to the study of NIN, Hyderabad, Kodo Millet contains the highest amount of folic acid (39.99 mg) among all the millets.

8. Proso Millet:

Proso Millet is far ahead in terms of a few nutrients among millets. It has the highest protein (12.5 g), magnesium (153 mg), riboflavin (0.28 mg), and niacin (4.5 mg) per 100 gm of grains (Source: Indian Food Composition Table 2017 - National Institute of Nutrition).

9. Browntop Millet:

Compared with rice and wheat, Browntop Millet has high nutritional value. It is rich in fiber, iron, calcium, potassium, magnesium, and many other important minerals. Browntop millet contains rich protein (11.5 g), an excellent amount of fiber (12.5 g), minerals (4.2 g), iron (0.65 mg), and calcium (0.01 mg) per 100 gm of grain.

The takeaway from this section on the Nutritional Value of Millets:

Every millet is unique in its nutrient content. Focusing on the rich content of the particular millet and building a product will attract more consumers and an association will develop gradually. Here are the nutritive values of millets:

Sl. No.	Nutrient	Millet	Nutritive value per 100 g.
1	Protein	Proso Millet	12.5 g
		Foxtail Millet	12.3 g
2	Iron	Pearl Millet	6.42 mg
		Barnyard Millet	5 mg
3	Zinc	Barnyard Millet	3 mg
4	Magnesium	Proso Millet	153 mg
5	Calcium	Finger Millet	364 mg
6	Fat	Pearl Millet	5.43 g
7	Dietary Fiber	Pearl Millet	11.4 g
8	Folic acid	Kodo Millet	39.4 µg
		Sorghum	39.42
9	Phosphorous	Foxtail Millet	290 mg
10	Carbohydrate s	Foxtail Millet	60.2 g

Three

HEALTH BENEFITS OF MILLETS

Before I start today, I will simply ask you a question from my heart.

Do you eat millet?

If you are health conscious and truly care about yourself and your family, you can definitely opt for millets and include them in your regular diet.

It was a time when millets were part of people's diets during the 1960s. But slowly the millets started disappearing from our plates and moreover referred only to rice and wheat and that too refined based cereals. Between 1962 and 2010, India's per capita consumption of millet fell drastically from 32.9 to 4.2 kg, while that of wheat almost doubled from 27 to 52 kg. (www.indiaspend.com). This led to less diversity in our regular food.

Have you ever heard of your grandparents suffering from lifestyle diseases like diabetes, obesity, and cardiovascular diseases? I think the answer will be an absolute "" No"".

I am sure, after going through this section you will come to know about the amazing health benefits of millet.

1. Millets help in controlling diabetes:

As you know "" seeing is believing"". In the year 2019, my mother had to go for an eye operation and found that she was suffering from diabetes. The doctor refused to do the eye operation as the blood sugar level was beyond 200 after food. The situation was really challenging for me. My mother started taking millets in her regular diet and within 30 days the result was amazing. The eye operation was successful.

From that day, I had a belief and confidence from within and can say Millets are good for diabetes.

Millets play an important role in managing and controlling the blood sugar level in our bodies. Due to the high fiber content in millet, glucose is released into the blood in a very slow and steady manner. That means millet will not cause a sudden spike in blood sugar levels.

Now, let us understand the overall status of diabetes in India and around the globe. In India, as per a report, there are 77 million people who are affected by diabetes and which is the second highest in the world. As per the International Diabetes Federation, there are 463 million people who are affected by diabetes in the world. 10% of global health expenditure is spent on diabetes and it is also astonishing to see that 11,10,100 children and adolescents below 20 years have type 1 diabetes.

Seeing these estimated reports, it is concluded that Diabetes is a global emergency.

To give more evidence on how millets are good for diabetes, it is necessary to see the scientific study on millets. Recently in the year 2021, a systematic review and meta-analysis of the potential of millets for managing and reducing the risk of developing diabetes were done by a team of scientists from different countries. This analysis was done across different types of millets and the forms of processing and cooking.

From the analysis, it was found that long-term millet consumption showed a reduction in HbA1c, which is lower than a rice-based diet. This meta-analysis confirmed that the millets evaluated have strong potential in dietary management and prevention of diabetes.

More points to understand why millets are good for diabetes.

- Due to the presence of high dietary fiber, it takes more time for digestion.
- A person does not get hunger pangs between meals as it keeps them satiated for a longer time.
- Millets are composed of complex carbohydrates which digest slowly in the body.

Looking into the nutritional profile of millets, here are the 5 types of millets which you can choose for diabetes.

Sl.No.	Millet	Carbohydrates	Fiber Content	C/F Ratio
1	Barnyard Millet	65.6	13.6	4.82
2	Browntop Millet	61.37	12.5	4.90
3	Little Millet	65.6	7.6	8.63
4	Foxtail Millet	60.2	6.7	8.98
5	Kodo Millet	66.2	5.2	12.73

No doubt, millets are beneficial in managing and controlling diabetes. It can be included in the regular diet of non-diabetic people as a preventive approach.

2. Millets for Weight loss/ obesity:

Obesity is increasing at a fast rate because of lifestyle and unhealthy eating and giving more preference to refined cereal-based diets, including more packaged food that are high in sugar, salt, and fats and taking a more high-calorie diet with low nutrients. It is reported that obesity or being overweight is the major problem faced by city dwellers as compared to rural people.

In the first-ever large-scale survey conducted by ICRISAT, 15,500 people were interviewed on millet consumption in India. In this survey, it was found that the single reason for eating millet was due to health problems (30% of people responded) and the next reason was people wanting to lose weight accounting for about 15%. This shows that millets have the potential to help people in shedding their extra kilos/weight.

The specific contents in the millet triggering weight loss in the body are dietary fiber, calorie content, policosanols, and tryptophan.

Let us see the function of dietary fiber in the millets that helps in weight loss.

- Due to high dietary fiber, carbohydrate absorption is slowed and glucose tolerance is reduced.
- Dietary fiber helps in water absorption.
- It acts as a detoxifying agent and helps in binding of the toxins.
- Food transit time in the intestine is increased due to dietary fiber.

When it comes to weight loss, the calorie content of the food is crucial, and taking fewer calories than our body truly burns can help us in losing weight.

Policosanols are found in Sorghum that helps in reducing cholesterol in our body. Study shows that the presence of policosanols in food helps in weight loss. Basically, policosanols are a group of high molecular weight (20-30 carbon) aliphatic primary alcohols found in plant epicuticular waxes. Choosing whole grain is beneficial for our body as whole sorghum contains about 69.7 mg/100 gm of policosanols whereas polished sorghum contains about 9.8 mg/100gm.

The presence of Tryptophan in the Foxtail Millet is responsible for slower digestion and prevents us from taking excess calories in our diet and helps us in weight loss. Tryptophan is an alpha-amino acid that's involved in protein synthesis.

In a study, it was found that consuming millet reduced the body mass index (BMI) by 7% in people who were obese and overweight. The results were based on the consumption of 50 to 200 gm of millet per day for a duration of 21 days to 3 months.

3. Millets are good for celiac patients

Celiac disease is a digestive disorder that damages the small intestine, triggered by eating food containing gluten. Gluten is a protein found in wheat, rice, and many more grains. Gluten makes the dough elastic.

When someone with celiac disease eats gluten food, their body overreacts to the protein and damages the villi of the small intestine.

Celiac disease is found in 1 out of 100 people worldwide. So, millets are becoming a part of the diet of celiac patients.

4. Millet detoxifies the body

Millets contain phenols and antioxidants and it helps to clean up toxins from the body.

5. Helps to protect against heart diseases

Millets contain essential fats, just the right amount to give our body natural fat. This helps prevent fat from depositing over muscles and avoids high cholesterol, heart strokes, and heart-related diseases.

A study was led by ICRISAT with 5 organizations analyzing the data of 19 studies with nearly 900 people. The study showed that consuming millets reduced total cholesterol by 8%. There was nearly a 10% decrease in low and very low-density lipoprotein cholesterol and triacylglycerol levels in the blood. It was also found that consuming millets decreased blood pressure with diastolic blood pressure decreasing by 5%.

6. Millets help in preventing cancer
   Millets are effective in the prevention of cancer initiation and progression. Millets contain fibers and phytonutrients, the combination of which is believed to reduce the risk of developing colon cancer.

7. Millets help to slow the aging in the body

Everyone likes to look and remain young always. Millets are a good source of antioxidants. The high amount of antioxidants present in millets fights the free radicals present in the body which slows down the aging process.

8. Millets improve skin elasticity

Millets are rich in amino acids called L-Lysine and P-Proline. Millets help to create collagen in the body, a substance that gives structure to the skin and tissue. Thus eating millet fortifies the collagen level to improve skin elasticity and makes it less prone to wrinkles.

9. Millets help in preventing anaemia.

In India, Anaemia is prevalent and it is mostly found in children, pregnant and non-pregnant women. Millets are the best source of iron. Iron is beneficial in preventing anaemia. Pearl Millet (Bajra) contains the highest iron content (11 mg per 100gm grains). Consumption of Pearl Millet prevents iron deficiency in the body.

10. Millets help in reducing hypertension

Millets help in preventing the oxidation of low-density lipoprotein thus reducing hypertension.

11. Millets act as prebiotics and improve gut health.

We know that millets are rich in dietary fiber, both soluble and insoluble. The insoluble dietary fiber in millets is known as a prebiotic that supports bacteria in our digestive system.

Four

MYTHS AND BELIEFS ABOUT MILLETS

1. Millets are hard to cook and not tasty: It is very easy as we cook with rice and wheat. If proper steps and techniques are used, tasty and yummy recipes can be prepared with millets.

2. Millets are hard to digest: Millets contain high fiber and prevent constipation. As per my experience, soaking millets help in better digestion.

3. Millets are bird feeds: Millets are not only the bird's feed but also best for human consumption and it increases immunity in human beings. In western countries, millets were particularly grown for bird feed but today India exports to western countries for human consumption.

4. Millets are meant for poor people: Now millets have become rich man's foods. The demand for millets is increasing in urban areas. Due to modern lifestyles, health-related problems like obesity, diabetes, cardiovascular diseases, and hypertension are increasing in urban areas and millets can solve these problems.

PART- II
CURRENT TREND OF MILLETS

One

MILLET VALUE CHAIN ANALYSIS

To understand the millet value chain from farm to plate, we need to see the activities carried out under production, processing, and marketing. Each activity needs to be analyzed considering the parameters.

The parameters considered under production are the types of millets grown in different states of India, the land devoted for growing millets, suitability of climate, the package of practices followed by the millet farmers including organic and natural farming, availability and source of seeds, the cost involved in producing millets at farm level and the returns farmers get and finally the constraints faced by the farmers.

Under processing will be covering the current millet processing technologies and the machines available in India, the output quality of the processed millets, stakeholders involved in procurement in different states, the standard of the value-added products, and lastly the constraints faced by the processors.

The marketing segment will be analyzing the parameters like the available value-added products in the market, pricing of the products, profit margins, and channels used for the distribution and promotion of the millet products.

Apart from the parameters involved in different activities, will also focus on support from the state and central governments, institutional technical support, incubation hand-holding support to the millet incubators, and awareness creation among the people.

Production:

In India, there are 9 types of millets grown by farmers. Most of the farmers are small and marginal farmers and it is preferably grown during the Kharif season depending upon the rain. Every state has some prominent millet growing areas or we can say millet corridors.

Let us see, what are the millets grown in different states, so that it will help us to build the backward market linkages.

Sl. No.	State	Millets grown
1.	Rajasthan	Bajra/Sorghum
2.	Karnataka	Sorghum/Ragi
3.	Maharashtra	Ragi/Sorghum/Little Millet
4.	Uttar Pradesh	Bajra
5	Haryana	Bajra
6	Andhra Pradesh	Sorghum, Ragi, Little and Proso Millet
7	Tamil Nadu	Ragi, Bajra, Little, Proso, Barnyard, and Kodo
8	Kerala	Sorghum, Finger Millet
9	Telangana	Bajra, Sorghum

10	Chattisgarh	Kodo Millet, Little Millet
11	Assam	Foxtail Millet, Ragi
12	Madhya Pradesh	Kodo Millet, Little Millet, Sorghum
13	Gujarat	Sorghum, Bajra, Finger Millet
14	Uttarakhand	Barnyard Millet, Finger Millet, Proso Millet

From the above data, you can get a clear picture of millet growing areas in India and help you in procuring raw materials for your startup.

It is seen that minor millets are grown by the tribal farmers and it is their source of food and sustaining livelihood. In recent days, it has been seen that farmers cultivating millets, mostly prefer Finger Millet, Sorghum, and Pearl Millet in their regular diet because these 3 millets are easy to process as compared to other minor millets.

With respect to the global scenario as per the report of FAO statistics, 2021, the millet area of India is 138 lakhs hectares and the production is about 173 lakhs tonnes. It shows that 80% of Asia's and 20% of global production, millets are produced in India. It is also very encouraging to see that India's average yield (1239 kg/ha) is better than the global (1229 kg/ha).

After the Green Revolution, the area under millets drastically reduced (56%) but the productivity has increased (228%) many folds and the credit goes to the development of technologies in this millet sector. But it is also an alarming situation where the diversity of millets has lost from 20% of the total food grain basket to 6% and this was dominated by wheat and rice.

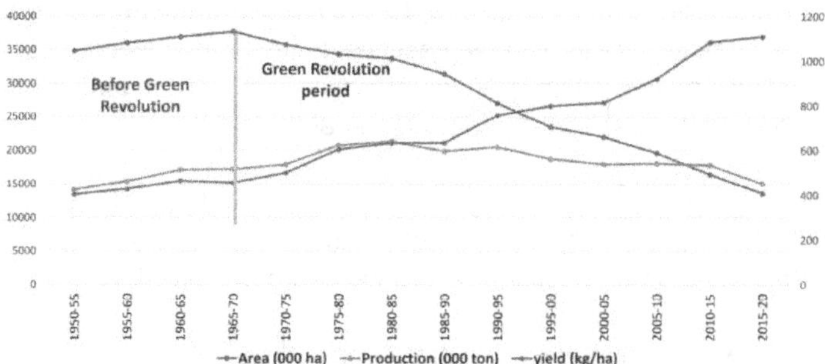

(Quinquennial Mean Area, Production and Yield of Millets in India)
Source: IIMR, Hyderabad

All millets can be grown in any type of soil, even in infertile soil the yield is better but few are resistant to water logging. Sorghum grown in Kharif is not used as food grain due to the incidence of developing grain molds.

Basically, Sorghum grown in the Rabi season is used as food. Millets grow well in dry areas of temperate, subtropical, and tropical regions and have the power to resist drought. Minor millets require low water and can fit into the small duration cropping window and it's an ideal crop to provide food and fodder security to the local farmers.

Although the hybrid seeds of Sorghum and Pearl Millet have come into the private seed chain, there is still a shortage of minor millet seeds. Most of the farmers use the seeds retained from the previous season. In the case of Finger Millet, the farmers are very well acquainted with the names of the varieties, even the high-yielding varieties.

In most cases, the farmers simply plow their land at the onset of monsoon and broadcast their seeds adding some Farm yard manure (FYM) and few apply chemical fertilizers. It has been noticed that the millets are highly responsive to chemical fertilizers.

The farmers following good agronomic practices get better yields as compared to traditional practices. It has been observed that following the System of Millet Intensification (SMI) in Finger Millet the yields go up to 8-10 quintals per acre.

While I was doing my project on "Utilization of Finger Millet in Nutritional Security" in Koraput I found some amazing facts to increase the production and productivity of Finger Millet.

- Awareness creation on the system of millet intensification (SMI) of finger millet as this method is giving more yields as compared to traditional methods.
- Conservation of local promising varieties which are giving more yields and sustaining from climate change.
- Giving more priority to weed control as it is the main constraint in Finger Millet production.
- Sowing/transplanting in time will enhance the production and productivity of finger millet.
- More production of finger millet will bring change in the livelihood of the tribal's by addressing the consumption part and also by selling in the market/mandi.
- Farmers must be encouraged to use the finger millet residue as fodder as it contains more nutrients and fiber.
- Development of context-specific improved varieties to improve productivity, increase shelf-life, improved nutritional content, and promote crop diversity.

For cultivation of a one-acre millet farm, the cost of cultivation ranges from Rs.12,000/- to Rs.20,000/- and if the farmers get a better price in the market, the profit may range from Rs.10,000 to Rs.30,000/-.depending upon the soil fertility and agronomic practices followed.

Processing of Millets:

The different shape, size, and color with wide variations make the primary processing of millets a challenge. Processing involves removing the minor millets' outer husk entirely as it is not fit for human consumption with minimal removal of bran without damaging the kernel and the germ.

There are many steps involved in the primary millet processing, starting from pre-cleaner, destoner, huller, grader, gravity separator, and finally packaging. If we take 100 kg of unhulled millet grains, the output of processed grains will be about 65-70 kg.

In addition to millet primary processing, in some units, the millet grains are completely polished, almost removing the bran and this makes the grains nutritionally poor. Even color sorting machines are used to segregate the millet grains uniformly depending upon the color and also any presence of impurities is removed.

After processing the grains, it is packed in 1 kg poly pack and for bulk order, it is packed in 25kg sacks. Some processing units also further do the secondary processing and make millet flour/mixed flour/ biscuits/cookies.

Marketing of Millets:

Price Spread in Millets Grains

FARMER PRICE
Rs.20/-
FACTORY PRICE
Rs.50/-
WHOLESALER PRICE
Rs.60/-
RETAIL PRICE
Rs.80/-

Millet procurement and marketing happens both in the public and private domain in different states. Odisha procures Ragi under Odisha Millet Mission from the farmers at Minimum Support Price (MSP) and in Chhattisgarh Little Millet and Ragi are procured from the farmers by the Forest Development Corporation.

In the private domain, the traders buy millets at different rates. For Ragi, it is about Rs.22 to Rs.24/- and Little Millet is purchased at Rs. 28 to Rs.35/-. After procuring millets, they are supplied to large processors in Karnataka, Andhra Pradesh, and Maharashtra.

The presence of a long chain of agents, traders, brokers, wholesalers, and millers add more prices to millets without any value addition and finally, the end consumers have to bear more prices for the processed products. This high price can only be minimized if procurement and marketing are done by Farmer Producers Organizations (FPOs) and subsequently FPOs are connected with the millet entrepreneurs.

After understanding the needs and preferences, millet entrepreneurs can develop millet products. It can be done by doing proper market and consumer research. Once the millet products are developed, different marketing strategies and approaches may be followed to reach the end consumers.

Two

MILLET CONSUMPTION TRENDS IN CURRENT AND FUTURE CONTEXT

It has been reported that the consumption of millets in Indian households has decreased. The per capita consumption of millets fell drastically from 32.9 kg to 4.2 kg from 1962-to 2010 (Source: Assessing Millets and Sorghum Consumption Behaviour in Urban India: A Large-Scale Survey, 2021).

The main reasons were the weak value chain of millets including the processing of millets, shelf life, entrepreneurs being unaware of the support from the government, and also there less development of millet value-added technologies.

But it has been observed that after the COVID-19 pandemic there is a rise in the consumption of millets in urban areas and also the demand for millets has gone up significantly across the globe since the breakout of the Russia-Ukraine conflict as Russia and Ukraine have banned the export of millets and its by-products.

There are a few states who have come forward to include millets in the Public Distribution System, mid-day meals in the schools, and ICDS programs. This initiative has marked an increase in millet consumption in rural areas.

There are many factors that have helped in the rise of millet consumption in urban areas. Let us see the most appropriate ones.

1. Convenience-seeking products
2. Health-Conscious consumers
3. Increasing Urbanization
4. Rise in disposable Income
5. Acceleration of e-commerce

In the present and future context, millets are becoming the main ingredients of products due to their versatile properties and richness in nutrient contents. Let us see the trends where millets will be playing an important role.

1. **Digestive wellness:** Millets are rich in fiber that contains both soluble and insoluble fiber. As you know, the insoluble fiber in millet acts as a prebiotic and it supports good bacteria in the digestive system. The presence of fiber combats constipation.

2. **Gluten-free products:** Millets being 100% gluten-free, makes its presence in the products suitable for celiac patients. The gluten-free trend is increasing in India and also abroad. In the United States, it is adopted at an 8-10% rate.

3. **Plant-based products:** In the world of plant-based food technology, there is always the search for new plant ingredients with useful functional properties, exceptional flavors, and sustainable benefits to create plant-based alternatives to animal products like meat and milk. Millet is rich in protein and can cater to the need for protein in our body and also the milk extracted from millets can reduce the dependency on animals.

4. **Snackification:** For a long time, snacking had been associated with unhealthy foods like deep-fried and loaded with high amounts of salt and sugar. But now

there is a paradigm shift towards a healthy snack version.
According to the Godrej Food Trends 2022, report, 55.6 percent of the culinary panel predicted a growing desire among the people to rediscover cultural roots and support locals through food and 55.6 percent predicted millet-based snacks will be in demand.

5. **Sportification:** The sportification trend will continue to influence a wide range of food and beverages as consumers are looking for protein as well as healthy and safe energy to reach their goals. So, the product developers will have to work with functional ingredients to develop food such as snack bars and plant-based beverages that will deliver sustained energy for both mental and physical performance.
   Millets have the ability to act as functional ingredients to fit into the upcoming sportification trend.

6. **Personalisation:** The trend of personalization can be seen in everything from entertainment to food. You might have heard a song on Spotify. They provide a personalized curated song list as per your choice and interests. In the same way, it works on food taking the data of the consumers and the problems faced by them. It gives the users a better experience because it requires no conscious input and involves no effort from the users. The products made from millet ingredients can solve the problem of the consumers in a better way.

7. **Good Carbs Bad Carbs:** Carbohydrates are naturally found in plant-based foods and these are typically good carbs, this type of carb is called complex carbs. Complex carbs break down more slowly allowing a more gradual release of energy.

   But bad carbs are simple carbs that convert to sugar at a much faster rate that can spike blood sugar in our body.

Complex carbs promote a healthy digestive system, regulate hormones, support weight loss, and provide sustainable energy.
All millets contain complex carbohydrates and come under the category of good carbs.

Three

GOVERNMENT INITIATIVES IN PROMOTING MILLETS IN THE NATIONAL AND INTERNATIONAL LEVEL

Since 21st June 2015, the International Year of Yoga is celebrated annually across the world. India took Yoga internationally and in the same way, 2023 has been declared the International Year of Millets. That happened when 72 other countries supported the proposal of India to the United Nations. It is a proud moment for India and at the same time a huge responsibility to lead.

Importance of Millets:

In the year 2018, the Government of India celebrated the National Year of Millets, and in the same year, the coarse cereals-Millets were notified as Nutri-Cereals due to their high nutritional value. The importance of millets was much more felt during and after the COVID-19 pandemic as these grains contain a high density of nutrients including minerals, vitamins, and dietary fiber.

Aim of the International Year of Millets:

The aim of celebrating 2023 as the International Year of Millets is as below:

- Elevate awareness of the contribution of millet to food security and nutrition.
- Inspire stakeholders on improving sustainable production and quality of millets.
- Draw focus on enhanced investment in research and development and extension services to achieve the other two aims.

Do you think the aims that have been put forth are being rightly carried out??

India is moving in the right direction by taking a lot of initiatives. Recently India's Prime Minister Narendra Modi highlighted the benefits of millet in his "Mann ki Baat" radio program.

"Millets are beneficial for the farmers and especially the small and marginal farmers. Millet crops do not require much water and get matured in a very short period. Millets contain plenty of protein, fiber, and minerals. Many people even call it a superfood. Along with reducing obesity, they also reduce the risk of diabetes, hypertension, and heart-related diseases. Millets are also very beneficial in fighting malnutrition since they are packed with energy as well as protein."

This message has reached millions of people and created mass awareness of the importance of millet.

Initiatives for the International Year of Millets:

The Ministry of Agriculture and Farmers Welfare has launched many initiatives in the run-up to the International Year of Millets to create awareness among the people in India. The Ministry of Agriculture is the nodal agency and the Indian Institute of Millets Research has been made the nodal institute for the celebration of the International Year of Millets. India is taking the lead in popularizing the theme in a strong manner at the international level through various campaigns. Let us take a look at these campaigns.

Mighty Millets Quiz:

10 questions in 300 seconds. The questions are based on millets and their benefits. The best thing is that participants from all over the world and of all nationalities are eligible to participate in the quiz. The day the quiz came in front of me, I immediately jumped to take the quiz. Answered all the questions wholeheartedly and was happy to receive the certificate.

India's Wealth, Millets for Health -Comic Story Contest:

The Ministry of Agriculture and Farmers' Welfare along with MyGov launched a contest for citizens to share their creativity by designing a comic story to showcase millet benefits and raise awareness among the masses. Selected entries will be amplified on social media and 100 selected winners will get certificates. This contest is open to the entire world.

Mapping and Exchange of the Good Practices (MEGP) for Millets Mainstreaming in Asia and Africa:

On 19th July 2022, NITI Aayog and World Food Program have taken initiative for Millets mainstreaming in Asia and Africa. In this context, a compendium of good practices will be prepared for scaling up the production and consumption of millets.

It's a nice initiative by NITI Aayog and World Food Program and hoping that organizations and practitioners from government or non-government organizations, multilateral or FPOs/SHGs/PACS/Cooperatives and private sector/startups will participate wholeheartedly with a case story of the intervention that has been conceptualized and implemented in some geography in Asian and African countries.

Millet Startup Innovation Challenge:

This Innovation Challenge was launched on 10th September 2022 to encourage young minds by nurturing their creative thinking and innovative strategies in the millet sector to address the concerns and create new techniques to position millets as alternative staples across the world. The startups, researchers, and students providing technological/business solutions in the following areas are eligible to participate.

- Improvement in dehulling efficiency and separation.
- Improvement of the shelf life of the millet-based product.
- Innovative millet-based products- Innovative packaging.
- Application of AI, ML, and blockchain in Millet business.

In today's millet sector scenario, the above are the important areas where most of the Millet Startups are facing problems. If proper solutions are brought forward, it will open up opportunities for many entrepreneurs and I am sure huge investments will be coming in the future.

Funds for Research and Development of Millet Incubation Center:

Finance Minister Nirmala Sitharaman announced providing Rs.25 crores under the NABARD's rural infrastructure development fund to the University of Agricultural Science (UAS), Raichur, Karnataka for the establishment of an incubation center for processing and value addition for the promotion of millets.

Interactive Session with Millet Start-ups and Entrepreneurs under International Year of Millets:

On 1st September 2022, a meeting was held under the chairmanship of Secretary, Department of Agriculture and Farmers' Welfare, MoA & FW at Krishi Bhawan, New Delhi with Millet Startups and Entrepreneurs. I had the opportunity to attend this meeting and shared my views. Important issues of the Millet Sector and challenges faced by Startups were discussed briefly and action points were formulated as given below.

- Meetings with embassies of relevant countries in India for promoting millets.
- Supporting startups to travel to International events and countries' embassies.
- Work with the trading arm of embassies for millet exports and standardization.
- Millet park on a PPP mode.
- Funding for running a millet-based experience center.
- Placement of millet products in big retail stores and e-commerce platforms.
- Establishing Labs in agricultural colleges

National Nutri Cereals Convention 4.0:

I had the opportunity to attend the National Nutri cereal convention 4.0 held on 23-24, September 2022 at HICC, Kondapur, Hyderabad. It is the largest convention bringing multi-stakeholders under one roof. It is a flagship event of ICAR-IIMR conducted by Nutrihub every year in Hyderabad, Telangana. The objective of the convention was to bring together all the stakeholders from Nutri Cereals Industry, from producers to processors to consumers, as well as academicians, researchers, and policymakers.

Hope the events, campaigns, and investments in the Millet sector will increase awareness among the masses and bring a remarkable change in the millet ecosystem by involving different stakeholders.

International Year of Millets Focus Areas of Odisha Millet Mission:

Odisha Millet Mission has been appreciated at the national and international levels for promoting millets. Odisha has received the award for the second time in the National Nutri-Cereals Convention held at Hyderabad. Previously the award was for the Best Millet promoting State and this time for Best State for scaling up Millet Mission.

Preparation for the International Year of Millets is in full swing and Odisha is taking a lot of initiatives in promoting and bringing awareness among the people. The focus areas are

- Benchmarking Sustainable Development Goals (SDGs) and Millets. 41 sub-indicators have been identified. Data-driven SDG framework of millets to be evolved for creating sustainable finance investment.

- Documentation of the Food Culture of 62 tribes of Odisha.
- Millet tradition to be integrated with tribal museums.
- Massive consumer awareness of ancient grains with chefs and interns.
- Expert committee was formed to transform each aspect of the Odisha Millet Mission into a gender-inclusive intervention.
- Celebration and co-branding of the International year of millets and Hockey World Cup and different sporting events at the state and district level.

CHAKH LE MILLETS: Branding of IYOM-2023 and Hockey World Cup of Odisha Millets Mission.

PART - III

MILLET BUSINESS IDEAS WITH SUCCESS STORIES

One

MILLET VALUE ADDITION

In this section, I will be telling you about successful millet startups that started from scratch and today they are able to reach millions with their belief in the millet grains and building relationships with the end users.

Who said millets cannot be tasty?

This was rightly proved by Prashant Parameswaran a young, Kochi millet entrepreneur who packed Ragi into tasty, delicious, healthy breakfast options with the Soulful brand. The journey of entrepreneurship started in the year 2013.

Let me introduce his background and what made him choose millet for his startup. Prashant comes from an agrarian background and did his MBA from Babson College Massachusetts. After completing his MBA he joined the agro-food industry and spent a few years, where he studied consumer trends deeply as he dealt with more than 20 different categories of food products.

It was the time when Quinoa was in demand in western countries and had come to India too. That raised Prashant's interest to work on our Indian ancient grains which are nowadays called

Nutri-Cereals. This interest and thought led to the founding of Soulfull to deliver millet innovative products in India.

From the beginning, it managed to maintain an edge over its competitor products with the use of Nutri-cereals as grains are a rich source of fiber and other micronutrients. He makes millet products that are focused on the Health and Wellness food segment with a portfolio of products for children and adults. The innovative millet products are ragi bites, millet muesli in different variations, and an instant multigrain drink mix.

Tata Consumer Products Limited (TCPL), the consumer products company of the Tata Group comprising beverages and foods, announced the 100% acquisition of Kottaram Agro Foods, the owner of Soulfull. The company has agreed to acquire 100% of the issued and paid-up equity share capital of Kottaram Agro Foods for consideration of Rs.155.8 crore. In February 2021, Tata Consumer Soulfull Private Limited became a 100% subsidiary of Tata Consumer Products. The acquisition has not only enhanced the brand's credentials with consumers but also provided an opportunity to spread the goodness of millet by making them more mainstream.

Even today I can find Soulfull products in the interior rural retail shops and that's the power of Tata brand outreach. Tata Consumer Products currently has a reach of around 2.4 million outlets.

Post-pandemic, there was a rise in the sale of millet products as more people were understanding the importance of building immunity through lifestyle changes. As Tata Soulfull has bought these ancient grains into the consumers' plates in more suitable and convenient forms, this has attracted loyal end consumers.
The recent integration of the Tata logo with the Soulfull brand across online platforms, marketing collaterals, and packaging has enhanced its brand credibility.

Prashant believes that to make millet more attractive to consumers there is a need to bring innovative millet products without compromising the taste and nutritional benefits. When a product matches the expectations of the people, there is huge acceptance and Tata Soulful can offer value to the end consumers.

The presence of Tata Soulfull products on their digital platforms is gaining a lot of traction which is enabling them to engage with the consumers directly and is providing better brand conversations. In the coming days, Tata Soulfull will continue investing in the targeted brand communication campaigns said, Prashant.

I was hearing to Prashant Parameswaran in a webinar, and want to share his thought on the Brand.
"I see a brand as a human being. Think of it as a child, think of it as the amount of life, and energy that one needs to be putting towards building the value system, building who the child is and essentially bringing the brand that consumers spend and buy into".

There is another Millet Startup that has sold more than 100 million millet units in just 3 years since its inception and with annual revenue of over Rs.70 crore with two rounds of funding.

Knowing the versatile nature of millet grains, in 2018 Raju Bhupati, Founder and CEO of Troo Good bought a tangible plan to bring out nutritious products using millets. He believes that taste largely drives the buying decision of most people, so it is an important factor to be addressed while making millet products.

Troo Good positioned its range of millet-infused nutritious bars and candies which is built on taste, affordability, and nutrition.
Bhupati says you need innovation to make it palatable and consumable so that it becomes a stable product in the market.

Troo Good offers various millet ready-to-eat products like Ragi/Millet Rusk, Multi Millet flour, Ragi flour, Vitamin chikkis using millets, Millet and dry fruit bars, and millet pop with a combination of honey and seeds.

Bhupati took efforts to infuse the peanut candy with millet which is 50 percent more nutritious than conventional peanut candy and it makes huge sales of 15-20 lakhs chikkis per day.

Bhupati maintains more than 200+ dedicated workforce. The company has developed strong linkages with farmers and FPOs to cater to better economies of scale.

Being a desi at heart, the idea of giving a modern twist to millets, to suit the needs of the always-on-the-run urban consumer, struck Krishnaa Kantthawala. Smart Eleven was born.

Smart Eleven currently offers a range of nutritious, tasty, easy-to-cook, and wholesome meals enriched with the goodness of millet. They offer healthier versions of comfort foods like noodles, pasta, Dalia, vermicelli, gluten-free khakhra, cookies, etc that are free of maida, monosodium glutamate (MSG), and preservatives. So, one can eat them guilt-free anywhere, any time of the day.

Consumers are very conscious about the food they eat today and the products of Smart Eleven have complete acceptance on the health and taste quotient across online channels, D2C, offline distribution, and even exports. Gauging the success of the millet products, they are in the process of introducing a range of over 23 different millet products including breakfast mixes, bakery products, energy bars, etc.

Applauding the commitment towards Millets, the Government of India has awarded Smart Eleven the 'Poshak Anaj'22' award for the Best Startup with the highest Grant amount from the Government of India under RKVY-Raftaar program supporting agripreneurs, via support from Nutrihub Incubation, IIMR.

Well, we don't again need the West to tell us that our ancient foods are the best way to keep us healthy, naturally. It is only upon us to drive this change and create a healthier India again, says Krishnaa.

Value addition is the process of taking a raw commodity and changing its form to produce high-quality end products. In the last decade, the demand for millet products has increased drastically in urban areas. The demand for convenience millet products like millet semolina, millet flakes, millet-based upma mix, millet weaning food, millet beverages, etc. is increasing because of changing lifestyles, socio, and economic patterns, an increasing number of working women, and modified food habits.

Millet technology has played an important role in making value-added products. Value addition makes the millet products convenient to cook and ready to eat. Millet products are nowadays easily available on online platforms, urban general stores, and supermarkets. It is also seen, exclusive organic shops are including processed organic millet products because people are becoming more conscious about their health.

Let us understand why millet value addition is required.

- To meet the taste/preferences of the consumers.
- Reducing post-harvest losses.
- Nutrient enhancement.
- Ready to eat (RTE), ready to Cook (RTC) – Reduces the cooking time.
- Enhance shelf life and make the product available for a long time.
- Diversified Millet products can solve our food needs as climate changes.
- Improving the consumption of millet products can help to overcome malnutrition.
- Millet farmers will have more post-harvest technologies thus enhancing the economic value of millet as well as improving the status of farmers.

MILLET PUFFS: Millet puffs are the product that is a result of explosive puffing where the millet grains are expanded to maximum expansion consistent with grain identity.

Before going to the millet puffs, let us understand the difference between popping and puffing.

Popping is a simultaneous starch gelatinization and expansion process, during which grains are exposed to high temperatures for a short time. During this process, the superheated vapor produced inside the grains by instantaneous heating cooks the grain and expands the endosperm suddenly, breaking out the outer skin.

You might have noticed that most people like to have popcorn while watching a movie and it is based on popping technology. It is an easy, simple, and low-cost technology as compared to puffing.

Puffing is a similar process to popping in which controlled expansion of the kernel is carried out, while the vapor pressure escapes through the micro pores of the grain structure due to high pressure.

Popping and puffing impart acceptable taste and desirable aroma to the snacks.

Though a wide range of cereals and millets such as rice, wheat, corn, sorghum, ragi, and foxtail millet are used for popping/puffing; only a few of them pop well. The reason behind this may be the factors that influence the popping qualities of cereals, such as season, varietal difference, grain characteristics such as moisture content, the composition of grain, and physical characteristics.

Gun puffing is a process in which the milled grains are introduced into the gun or high-pressure chamber after preheating, and then superheated steam is introduced to the closed rotating chamber (Luh,1991).

The steam pressure is critical to the final texture of the puffed product, as too low pressure would result in the product lacking crispiness and too high pressure would shatter the rice. Sufficient time is allowed for the superheated steam to cook the grain in a semi-plastic state and at the end, the pressure is suddenly released for obtaining the crispy puffed grain. Keesenberg (1978) developed a puffing gun, which was composed of a rotating horizontal cylinder having a length of 1.2 m and an inner diameter of 200 mm.

Millet puffs are ready-to-eat snacks that are developed using a puff gun machine. For making millet puffs, the millet grains are properly cleaned and graded using a grader-cum-cleaner. Then the grains are put into the dehuller for dehulling. Then the conditioning of dehulled grains is done using water and it is loaded in the puff gun machine rotating barrel under proper heat and pressure. The mixture is roasted and fried resulting in millet puffs.

Millet puffs are crispy and tasty. It has a shelf life of 2-4 months depending upon the type of millet and the packing materials used. Many ranges of millet products can be made by frying and coating with a different variant of masala. It can be served as premium products under the category of snacks.

MILLET RAVA/KHICHDI/ IDLI RAVA:

Millet Rava/Semolina is ready to cook food. It is made through milling technology where the bran and germ are separated from the starchy endosperm so that the endosperm can be ground into medium size Rava in a hammer mill.
The process starts with cleaning the grains and putting them into the feed. The grains are milled by the hammer crusher where the endosperm, germ, and bran get separated.
In this machine, we can get 3 variants of Millet Rava.
1. Fine Semolina (Idli Rava)
2. Medium Semolina (Upma Rava)
3. Coarse Semolina (Khichdi Rava)

Millet semolina has a shelf life of 3 months if packed properly and kept at ambient temperature. These millet products are an excellent source of complex carbohydrates, fiber, protein, calcium, iron, zinc, and magnesium.

MILLET PASTA AND VERMICELLI:
Pasta and Vermicelli are nowadays getting more demand in most households in India. But when it is made with millets, it's a healthier option. As it is a very quick and easy breakfast, we can make lots of recipes with the available vegetables at home.

To make pasta and vermicelli with machines, you need to follow some processes. It starts with mixing ingredients, extruding, drying/roasting, length sizing, and packing vermicelli. The machine which is used is called a single-screw extruder. It has three main parts- Die, Main Screw, and Mixing Screw.

Depending upon the output you have to change the die. For vermicelli, you need one die and for making pasta you need to change the die. The cost of the machine is Rs.11, 00,000/-. The capacity of the machine is 12 kilograms per hour.

The products are made with millet/sorghum flour or a combination of millet flour and semolina.

MILLET EXTRUDED SNACKS:
Extruded snacks can be made by using a twin-screw hot extruder. Most of the extruded snacks are prepared using corn. But taking millet as the main ingredient improves the nutritional value of the product. It can be done by mixing all the ingredients

and proper conditioning followed by mixing water and passing through the twin screw extruder and it results in expanded snacks that are ready to eat. The output snacks can be coated with special spices to give them a better flavor and taste.

MILLET FLAKES:

Most of us are familiar with cornflakes, but few know about millet flakes. Millet flakes can be made from most millets. For making flakes, the millets are cleaned properly and soaked in water overnight. Then it is roasted in a grain roaster. Then it is flattened to flakes using the edge-runner machine.

Millet flakes can be used for making breakfast items. It reduces the time of preparation.

MILLET ENERGY BARS:

Millet Energy Bars are one of the most demanded products in the market. It's very simple and easy to make. It can be made by mixing millet bran powder, millet flakes, or with millet puffs. The ingredients are mixed properly and the binding agents are added and put into shaping and finally cooling and packing the product.

MILLET LADDUS/ INSTANT LADDU MIX:

Laddus is one of the most popular sweets across India. It is mostly taken or made during festivals and special occasions. The main ingredients for making ladoos are millet flour, jaggery, some nuts, ghee, and cardamom for flavor.

Many variations of laddus can be made with millet.

I do remember when I made Ragi Ladoos without ghee and jaggery. It was superb and tasty and all the family members enjoyed it.

Making millet laddus and packing it up in beautiful boxes will become gifting boxes during festivals.

MILLET MUESLI:

Muesli is traditionally made with rolled whole grains by adding nuts, seeds, fresh and dried fruits, and often sweetener is added such as honey. Likewise, Millet muesli can be made by mixing millet flakes, dry fruits, roasted cashew nuts, almonds, pista, and raisins. After mixing it properly, it can be packed in beautiful packets.

Millet muesli can be used for breakfast, dessert, tasty snacks, and many more.

Two

MILLET MILK: AN ALTERNATIVE TO DAIRY MILK

Milk and other dairy products have been a major source of calcium for vegetarians but nowadays people are completely giving up animal products to turn into vegans. It is found that milk and dairy products are becoming harmful since commercialization. It has been reported that there is a rise in lactose intolerance in India and also abroad. People turn vegans out of choice and not because they are lactose intolerant.

The inability to digest the sugar in milk is called milk intolerance. With the help of an enzyme, lactase, lactose is broken into simple sugar in our body. But due to low levels of lactase in the body, the problem arises. The symptoms generally start 30 minutes to two hours after consuming milk. The symptoms are in the form of bloating, pain, cramps, gas, vomiting, and foamy stools.

The arising problem of milk tolerance gave birth to plant-based milk and that too from the ancient grains, millets. The process of extraction of milk from the millet is very simple and easy. In the ancient and today's world, most of us know the process of soaking and sprouting as we do with pulses. Soaking and Sprouting aid in easy digestion and simultaneously improve the availability of nutrients to be absorbed in the body.

Struggling to find plant-based milk for them and understanding the pain points of the consumers, Alt Foods developed plant-based milk made from grains and sprouted millets. The startup was founded by three family members Aman, Sweta, and Pavitra Khandelwal, who are on a mission to create easy-to-switch to plant-based products that are nutritious, great in taste, and accessible. India has the largest dairy consumption in the world and there is a tremendous market potential for plant-based alternatives in the country.

With the thought of taking plant-based alternatives to the masses, Alt Foods fills the appropriate gap and aims to make plant-based food more accessible to everyone.

While starting the startup they faced a lot of challenges as they were not having any prior experience. One of the biggest challenges was to create a novel dairy alternative without any benchmark product. The other thing was the scalability as the product was to be eventually affordable as dairy. But persistence and clarity helped them to achieve the right product.

Moving ahead with the right momentum and by putting in efforts, they launched plant-based milk products in two variants - original milk and chocolate-flavored milk. They could do it faster by participating in the ProVeg Incubator. It gave them more opportunities to connect with the right mentors, industry experts, and investors in one place.

Now their products are easily available on their own website and online aggregators and some retail stores in the Delhi NCR region. They are also planning to come with more plant-based milk flavors in the future as they see a huge shift in consumption where people have started rejecting the animal source food and are openly accepting plant-based products.

Three

MILLET-BASED HOTEL INDUSTRY AND MILLET CLOUD KITCHEN

With the advent of superfoods, millets are gaining popularity not only in Indian households' kitchens but also in hotels and restaurants. Nowadays millet-based hotels are mostly found in the major cities and day by day the numbers are increasing in Hyderabad, Bengaluru, Chennai, Mumbai, and many more. The millet menu is receiving appreciation and getting awesome responses from the people.

People can co-relate with their grandparents when they see age-old millet recipes on restaurant menus and happily try them, reliving their childhood memories.

Did you notice a change in the eating habits of the people post-COVID pandemic? Even when eating out, people are becoming increasingly health conscious.

So, if you are thinking of starting a millet-based hotel or restaurant, it is the right time to enter into the millet food business.

There are many who have entered into the millet-based food business and they are doing well in their space. To give you the right motive, I will be sharing two stories about people who have brought food sensations to the industry.

Recently, when M Venkaiah Naidu, the Vice President, who was on a visit to Visakhapatnam took to Twitter after his breakfast. He tweeted: ""'*Had a sumptuous breakfast of millet idlis today made by 'Vasena Poli' stall run by a young agri-entrepreneur Chittem Sudheer in Visakhapatnam"*. The tweet went viral.

In the year 2018, Chittem opened his first idli stall with an investment of Rs.50,000/- as ""Vasena Poli"" (meaning alternative idli) in Visakhapatnam. His day starts around 6:30 am, wrapping the idli batter in the cone-shaped Vistaraku leaf which is believed to have medicinal value, and putting it in a pot on the stove.

The uniqueness of the millet idli prepared by him has attracted people to him. He makes idlis with Jowar, Bajra, Kodo Millet, Foxtail Millet, Finger Millet, Barnyard Millet, Proso Millet, and Little Millet, and also serves chutneys made with peanuts, ginger, and vegetables. He sells more than 200 plates in a day and on average makes about Rs.15,000 at the end of the day. Despite the demand for his millet idlis, he has kept it very reasonable so that customers can easily afford it.

He is well connected with the millet farmers of the tribal belt in Visakhapatnam district and Parvathipuram in Vizianagaram district, where they are organically grown. He requires about 700 kg of millet grains every month which he procures from them.

He says, "After the COVID pandemic the number of customers has increased. Also after the tweet from the Vice President, he was flooded with requests from many places for expansion through franchises. He hopes to open more stalls in the city in the coming days.

Taking pride in introducing the ancient superfood grains into your meal plate as millet recipes, MILLET MARVELS has been started by Dr. Bharat Reddy in the pearl city of Hyderabad. It is a modern vintage kitchen offering delicious and tasty millet recipes. Soon after its opening in 2018, it is getting better responses and feedback from customers.

Bharat Reddy is a famous face in Telugu cinema. He is an actor and a cardiologist. Apart from his regular duty and responsibility he has the zeal to take millets to the people in the form of millet recipes and make awareness among the people on the nutritional and health benefits. This thought made him start Millet Marvels.

In the Millet Marvels, different types of millet dishes are served starting from dosa, idli, vada, puri, uthappam, and other food items made from different types of millets.

Dr. Reddy says it is not just doing business taking millet but simultaneously creating awareness among the people about the nutritional and health benefits. Today, Millet Marvels has branches across Hyderabad city at Film Nagar, Kismatpur, Manikonda, and Kapil Towers. In the coming future, he has a plan to expand Pan-India.

The concept of a cloud kitchen started a few years back in India and it has increased tremendously post-COVID. Cloud Kitchen is a commercially licensed kitchen for the purpose of preparing food for delivery or takeaways without dining space for customers. Millet-based Cloud Kitchen has tremendous potential growth when it is tied up with delivery partners in the cities like Swiggy and Zomato.

Recently, Apollo Hospitals has set up a cloud kitchen to serve millet-based food to patients in Jubilee Hills, Hyderabad. It will serve all the traditional Indian dishes made out of millet. In this connection, Apollo Hospitals has collaborated with the Indian Institute of Millets Research, Hyderabad for research. After extensive research and formulated palatable millet recipes are prepared for the patients. The millet recipes have played an important role in recovering patients in hospitals and this concept is bought by Dr. Bharat Reddy.

In recent days millet-based hotels and restaurants are coming up in urban areas. If you are planning to come up with such millet startups, it is the best time. Location and quality of food matter a lot in this food industry. You have to always keep this in mind while starting such startups.

Four

MILLET CUTLERY - IMPROVING HYGIENE AND SAVING EARTH FROM WASTE AND POLLUTION

You must have seen sign boards in airports claiming "Single-use plastic free airport". "Indira Gandhi International Airport" of Delhi is declared India's first single-use plastic-free airport and it has been certified by the CII-ITC Centre of Excellence for Sustainable Development.

Most plastics are not recycled globally and millions of tons of plastic pollute the world's oceans, impact wildlife and affect drinking water. Risk is associated with the tiny bits of broken-down plastics. According to the Federal pollution watchdog, in 2020, over 4.1 million metric tons of plastic waste was generated in India. You can imagine how severely it is impacting the environment.

So, to mitigate the pollution arising from plastics, spoons, and cutlery is being made with millets and you will be astonished to know that this millet cutlery is edible. This innovation has a better impact on society and also on the environment.

The main ingredients for making the cutlery are millet. As you know millets require fewer inputs and water, and a short period to grow, and thus helps farmers to sustain their livelihood through farming.

The innovation of millet cutlery was brought forward by Narayan Peesapathy, based in Hyderabad. He started his manufacturing business Bakeys Foods Private Limited in 2010. It was his day-night efforts experimenting with different ingredients that resulted in the final product. He has made a fully automatic edible cutlery manufacturing machine.

The idea of edible cutlery came to Peesapathy when he was having his food with a plastic spoon. Suddenly a thought came when he saw that the millet roti was just as hard as the plastic spoon and that he was able to scoop the curry with the jowar roti pieces. It was brittle but still edible. He has chosen jowar which is fairly neutral and allows different flavors to be mixed with it. The edible millet spoons are available in three different flavors: sweet, salty, and plain. To make the spoons delicious in taste he uses rock salt, cumin seed, and black pepper.

In the initial days, he faced a lot of challenges in marketing his product and it was difficult to make people believe in millet cutlery. The turning point of his business was when his video went viral on social media. From that point time to till today, there has been good growth and he can see the increase during and after the COVID pandemic when people are more particular with hygiene and cleanliness.

For this innovative product, Peesapathy has been awarded by Prime Minister Narendra Modi on World Environment Day for his contribution towards his "Swachh Bharat" mission.

In recent days, many startups are coming up with this concept of edible cutlery. Two women quit their lucrative job and started their startup in Bangalore. They manufacture eco-friendly, zero-waste edible cutlery made with millets and other ingredients under the brand name "EdiblePRO". Shaila Gurudutt and Lakshmi Bheemachar, founders of EdiblePRO offer 80 products of different variants in terms of designs, flavors, colors, and textures and most importantly at affordable rates.

With startups like Bakeys Foods and EdiblePRO actively acting against the plastic menace by providing eco-friendly alternatives, will definitely bring change in the environment and simultaneously will be a great help for the farmers in India.

Five

BIRD FEED INDUSTRY -MEETING THE NUTRITIONAL NEEDS OF PET BIRDS AND ANIMALS

In the 18th Century, Millets were cultivated in the United States of America mostly Foxtail Millet. It was used as bird feed in western countries. As you know, India is the highest producer of Millets and most of the millets were exported from India for bird feed.

Why are Millets good for Birds?

As we know millets are highly nutritious and rich in nutrients and their demand is increasing in every household in India and abroad. When it comes to bird feed, we need to select the right kind of grains so that the loved birds remain healthy without falling sick. During the COVID-19 pandemic period, due to bird feed shortage, a lot of people fed their birds cooked rice, puff rice, and other junk feeds which made the birds sick.

Now, let me say you why millets are considered as right feed for birds:

1. Millets are highly nutritious. They are rich in Magnesium, Phosphorous, and Calcium.
2. It is a healthy and palatable treat for the birds.
3. It is low in fat and high in good carbohydrates.
4. It contains high fiber so it is easily digestible.
5. Millets are weaning food for small birds.
6. The texture of millet grains is appealing to birds.
7. Millets are alkaline which counteracts the acids in birds.
8. Millets build the immune system in birds.
9. It acts as a natural stress reliever for birds.
10. It supplies essential vitamins like B1, B2, B3, and B6.

There is an opportunity in this sector. During the COVID-19 pandemic, I got a lot of queries about Proso Millet availability and supply from India and abroad. I got a call from a zoo too for the bird feed. Most of the millets which are exported from India are as Bird Feed.

If you are planning to start your millet startup in this segment, it will be a good idea.

The bird feeds segment is unorganized in India. The millet bird feeds which are available in the market are not properly cleaned or packed. To start a business in this sector, you need a cleaner-cum-grader machine, which may cost around Rs.1 to Rs.2 lakhs. Other than this you need a packaging machine.

Six

ESTABLISHING MILLET PRIMARY PROCESSING UNIT

Millets have a higher proportion of complex carbohydrates and the kind of protein that complement the types of protein found in plant and animal-based food items.

To start with, before starting a primary millet processing unit, it is very important to understand the structure of the millet and how to get maximum benefit by consuming the right processed millet grains. It is known to us that the lesser the Carbohydrate/Fiber (C/F) ratio, the better the grain. The C/F ratio of millets is much less than wheat and rice.

The fat and mineral content of millet is much higher in millets. In millets, all the fiber, minerals, and fats are concentrated in an intermediary layer of the grain and which is called the bran layer. So, it is always advisable to retain the bran layer as much as possible to derive the maximum nutritional benefits from millets.

Removing the husk while retaining the bran is a challenging job in millet processing. The more the bran layer is retained, the sooner the de-husked grains get damaged. It is also noticed that the more the husked grains are rubbed or impacted against the metal surfaces of the machines, the bran gets more damaged.

So, it is important to design our millet processing machines in such a way that the bran layer gets less damaged.

The more the content of fatty acids in millets, the faster is the chance of damage. The fatty acids determine the shelf life of the millets after processing.

We can keep the millet grains for more than a year, if the husk is intact and the moisture level is 11-12%. If the moisture level is above 13%, it needs to be dried properly and packed, and stored in a clean and warm place. It is found that when the millet husk is intact and dried well, there is no infestation of pests but when the grains are dehusked there are chances of attack of pests.

Once the millets are dehusked, the shelf life starts decreasing from the very day. So, care should be taken in every aspect to reduce the damage to the grains.

It was a day in 2019, when I visited a tribal village in Koraput, Odisha in search of a millet processing unit and could find a handcrafted traditional wooden chakki used for the processing of millets. It was astonishing to know that it was the single chakki in the entire village and had been made 15 years back.

The wooden chakki was interesting and I was curious to know how it worked and the mechanism behind it.

To set up a primary millet processing unit, we require machines for cleaning, grading, dehulling, and making value-added products. Let us discuss one by one of each machine.

Grader-cum-Aspirator:

Primary cleaning is done using a grader cum aspirator with the support of different sieve sizes for different millet grains. The grader separates the millet grains from sand particles, stones, sticks, mud balls, sticks, straws, etc. So selecting the right kind of sieve is an important factor to get good quality millet grains.

Before putting the millet grains into the machine, the moisture of the grains should be checked. It should be around 11-12% moisture level. Otherwise, we need to dry the grains in sunlight for 2-3 days for desired moisture level. Even solar dryers can be used for drying.

Proper care should be taken to prevent the millet grains from clogging. The machine operator can use a brush to remove the grains which are clogged into the sieve. For small millet processing, we generally use a triple deck grader with three sieves.

The top sieve will separate big stones, sticks, straws, etc. which are bigger than the millet grain. The middle sieve will separate the good-quality grains and the last sieve will separate the fine and coarse sand particles.

The aspirator attached to the grader will send the fine dust particles to the rear end.

Destoner:

The material coming from the grader is sent to the Destoner for removing the small stones and mud balls that are identical to the size of the grains. Destoner works on the principle of gravity. A Destoner has two sieves under the hopper which grade the material coming from the hopper. The graded material falls on the destoner bed where the lighter material moves towards the front and the heavier material moves towards the rear end.

The air adjustment slot has to be adjusted carefully depending on the material.

Dehuller-cum-Aspirator:

The raw materials after proper cleaning are sent for husk removal into the huller. Dehullers can be classified into two types under the millet processing machinery.

Centrifugal Dehullers:

A Centrifugal Dehuller has an impeller that is responsible for the husk removal. The material is sent to the hopper which then enters the impeller, where it gets thrown with a great centrifugal force onto the impeller casing. Due to the heavy impact, the husk gets separated from the millet rice and is sent to the aspirator where the lighter husk is collected at the back and the rice is collected at the front.

The quality of the dehuller is measured depending on the retention of the bran layer on the millet rice after dehulling.

Abrasive Dehuller:

Abrasive dehuller is classified into two types, one is the Emery type and the other one is Rubber roller type. In Emery type dehuller two grinding stones are used for husk removal, where one stone is stationary and the other rotates at a constant speed. The raw material passes through these two grinding stones and the husk gets sheared or abraded off.

In the Rubber roller type, rubber rollers are used instead of stones.

Millet Processing Machine Manufacturers in India:

- Perfura Technologies (India) Pvt. Ltd
- Small Millet Foundation (Division of DHAN Foundation)
- AVM Engineering Industries
- Agromech Engineers
- KMS Industries
- Borne Technologies Private Ltd.

Let me bring some of the initiatives taken by the Small Millet Foundation (Division of DHAN Foundation) in the millet processing sector.

Small Millet Foundation (Division of DHAN Foundation):
On 20th, September 2019, Madurai Symposium was conducted by DHAN Foundation at Tamukkam Ground, Madurai. I had the opportunity to present in a workshop on reducing the drudgery of women in processing small millet. On this day, the first Tabletop Millet dehuller was launched by M.P. Vasimalai, Executive Director of DHAN Foundation, and this machine was developed by Saravanan and his team as part of the scaling up of small millet post-harvest and nutritious food products.
The Millet Table Top Impact Huller-SMF V3 has many advantages:

- Processes all kinds of small millets.
- Higher head rice recovery.
- Can processes small quantities(even 0.5kg)
- Retention of more nutrients.
- Energy efficient.
- Compact, low weight and portable.
- Value for money.
- Safe, easy to operate, and maintain.
- Low noise.
- Ability to operate for long hours.
- Capacity: 30 to 80 kg/hr depending on the millet.
- Hulling efficiency: more than 90%

Today this machine has reached more than 76 millet farmer communities in 19 states. DHAN Foundation has been working since 2011 in small millet promotion including conservation, production, consumption, processing, value addition, marketing, and policy advocacy. As part of the research activity of Small Millet Foundation (A division of DHAN Foundation) regarding overcoming and processing small millets, they found out that hulling was the most challenging operation and came up with SMF Series Huller capable of hulling all small millets like Kodo, Browntop, Barnyard, Little, Foxtail and Proso Millet.

This machine could run on a single or three-phase electricity connection and in a very short period became very popular throughout the country.

In 2018 DHAN Foundation was approached by the North Eastern Region Community Management Project (NERCORMP) of Arunachal Pradesh with a specific objective of developing and innovating the existing machines to run on alternate sources of energy preferably driven by diesel or petrol as they had electric current supply problem in North-East.

Due to the inherent problem of diesel engines for more maintenance as engines seized and decided to work on petrol engines and in six months brought out petrol-driven table-top hullers, commercial portable hullers, and commercial pulverizers. These machines were as efficient as the electric version. But facing some unforeseen problems as these machines needed pure petrol to start and would not start with spurious petrol available in most petrol pumps in Arunachal Pradesh. The number of petrol pumps in the North East is very less and far away from millet growing villages. There was also difficulty in carrying petrol to high mountainous villages having no roads. During the annual General Body Meeting of the Small Millet Foundation, this problem was discussed and came up with an idea that going with solar-powered machines will solve the problem of many remote villages and will be a climate-smart solution.

Under the guidance of Dr.Dayakar Rao, Principal Scientist, IIMR started working on it and succeeded in bringing out the prototype solar dehuller. This machine was tested and passed all critical parameters and was ready for commercial launch.

The advantage of this huller is that it can run on electric, solar, and battery power. This 0.5 HP motor is installed with a solar panel, battery backups, and an inverter to convert the energy. The battery backup is enough to run the machine continuously for 4 hours in the absence of an electric supply or solar energy. So, the unit is simple, easy to operate, and efficient and it is proven to be a boon for remote small millet farmers and processors.

The person behind all of this initiative is Saravanan, professionally an Agri Engineer. He joined DHAN Foundation and worked in Maharashtra implementing Convergence of Agricultural Interventions Maharashtra (CAIM) distressed districts for four years and then moved to Tamil Nadu and worked on the above project. He is using efficient food value chain technology to promote ecologically feasible nutritious millet grains and further catalyze food diversity.

With the increase in demand for these millet machines and requests for higher capacity, DHAN has come up with a 750-1000kg/hr Commercial Millet huller.
All DHAN huller models (tabletop, portable and Commercial) are available at IIMR, Hyderabad.

Let us see what are the millet processing machines and infrastructure required to establish a Millet Processing unit at different levels with different capacities.

1. **Village/Community Level**: You require a space of 200 square feet floor area. Destoner-cum-Grader with Aspirator and a Dehuller is sufficient. It may cost around 2 lakhs. Tabletop dehuller which costs around Rs.75, 000/- will fit into this project. Its capacity is around 50kg/hr and two-person can easily operate it. It can work in a single phase.
2. **Small Scale Level:** It requires a minimum of 1200 square feet of floor area to operate the machines. Destoner, Grader, and Dehuller two numbers each are required. Its capacity is around 100 kg/hour. It may cost around 4-5 lakhs.
3. **Medium Scale Level:** The capacity of this enterprise may be around 500-1000 kg/hour.

5000 to 10,000 square feet is required with godowns to stock raw materials up to 10-20 tonnes. In this enterprise, we can keep Destoner and Grader of four to eight numbers, Two to four dehuller machines. For value addition, we can keep Pulveriser, Semolina Machine, and Flakes Making Machine. It cost maybe around 20-30 lakhs.

4. **Large Scale Level:** Most of the large-scale Enterprises are found in Nashik. It may cost around Rs.60-70 lakhs to Rs.1 Crore.

Seven

MILLET BAKERY UNIT

Are you eating healthy biscuits or cakes?

Most of the biscuits or cookies or cakes available in the market are made of refined flour and the ingredients used in making them are unhealthy. I am sure most of the health-conscious people who buy any product would look at the ingredients before buying it. But have you ever seen people looking at the ingredients that are used in the cakes? In most places, the ingredients are not mentioned.

But making bakery products with millet will give healthy options to people. The demand for ready-to-eat convenience products is steadily increasing. Entrepreneurs are coming up with tasty, healthy biscuits made from powdered millets, and dry fruits, and instead of using refined sugar and oil, they are using jaggery, butter, or ghee or even going completely vegan and gluten-free.

Apart from these, people find it healthy because it is gluten-free and free from baking powder, baking soda, eggs, added flavor, preservatives, and additives.

So, to start a millet bakery unit, you require three machines. The procedure of making biscuits/cookies start with creaming, mixing with millet flour in a planetary mixer, dough making, rolling, cutting into the required shape in an automatic cookie cutting machine, and finally baking, cooling, and packing. The three machines are-

1. Planetary Mixer
2. Cookies cutting machine
3. Rotary Convection Oven.

Planetary Mixer:

Planetary mixers are generally used for making cakes, biscuits, cookies, bread, buns, etc. This machine consists of a kettle, blades, and a kettle shifter. There are different blades for making cakes, biscuits, breads, and a scraper. In the food processing industry, it is suitable for mixing the solid and liquid ingredients.

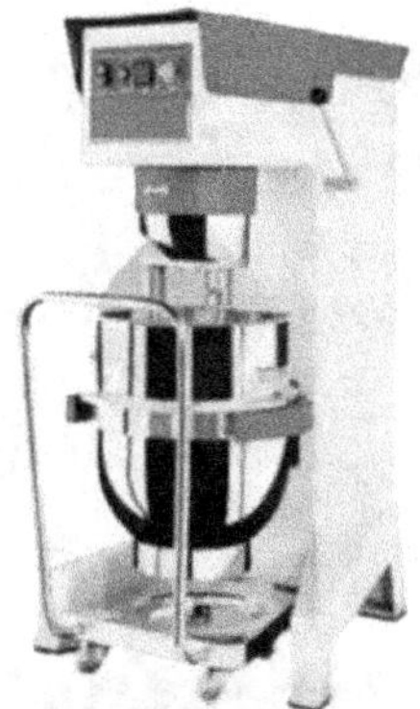

Millet Planetary Mixer

Before selecting a planetary mixer, it is always advisable to go with one which is designed to comply with hygiene and safety regulations. You can also look for a machine that has the facility to inject air while mixing which reduces the mixing time and enables the provision of aerated dough.

Apart from these features, it must have a speed adjuster and height adjuster for the blades.

The planetary mixer comes with different capacities starting from 8 kilograms to 175 kilograms and you can go as per your requirement.

Cookies cutting machine:

The cookie-cutting machine consists of a hopper in which sheeting rollers are inserted and beneath the rollers cutting die are fitted. The function of the sheeting rollers is to spread the dough into a biscuit shape. The machine is digitally controlled. As per the command and setting instructions, the dough is cut into the required shape. There are many models for making cookies like straight drop, twist drop, drag-drop, drag-twist drop, and wire cut.

Millet Cookie-Cutting Machine

In this machine, there is a sensor that can sense the tray once it is placed and cut the dough into the given command.

Different shapes and adding flavor to the cookies will increase the number of product ranges and also consumers will be attracted to them. Early Foods and Tots and Moms make different ranges of millet cookies.

Rotary Convection Oven:

If you have a convection oven at home, you would know that a rotary convection oven is better than a plain convection oven. The warm air in the convection oven is not dispersed evenly. Whereas in a rotary convection oven, the trays are rotated while a built-in fan circulates warm air around the food being cooked. As a result, a rotary oven cooks food more quickly and at a lower temperature than a convection oven. The components of the rotary oven are a cabin with racks, trays, an oven cavity, and a temperature indicator on the starter.

Hope this has given you a general idea of how to start a millet bakery unit and the machines required. Apart from this, I want to share one more inspiring entrepreneurship journey around millets in the baking business.

Natasha Gandhi, the founder and owner of the "House of Millets" makes bakery products with millets without using refined sugar, dairy, and refined flour. This startup was started in January 2019 and it is located at Mulund West, Mumbai.
It offers a variety of millet-based cakes that are completely vegan and gluten-free. There are different types of cakes on the menu of the House of Millets such as Burst Cakes, Pull-me-up cakes, Tea cakes, etc. In addition to that, she offers brownies, flavored cupcakes, and muffins.

Looking back, Natasha was one of the top 5 contestants in MasterChef India season 6. She was called to the audition for the show which she thinks is all due to House of Millets.

The idea of starting this startup came when she was unable to find a good bakery where she was staying. Even those who were present were charging a huge amount for the cake and also for delivering it. After the proper survey, she could figure out that there is a need for healthy bakery products. Also selecting millet as the main ingredient came to her mind when her father was diagnosed with diabetes. So many reasons made her make healthy cakes with millet and other ingredients.

Although she makes cakes with different types of millet, her favorite is Sorghum because it is super versatile in handling and the taste is very close to the regular wheat flour. After many trials and errors, she could find the best binding agents like flax and chia seeds for making cakes.

Today there is a huge demand for cakes from House of Millets and every day they take orders and deliver them to the people in Mumbai. They find repeat customers coming to them as the cakes taste awesome and healthy.

As the International Year of Millets will be celebrated in the year 2023, she looks at MasterChef India to introduce a millet-based round for the next season which will bring more awareness and increase the reach of millets.
Leaving a note for all the entrepreneurs, Natasha says, "*Do what you love and always follow your passion*".

Eight

MILLET BABY FOOD PRODUCTS

Every parent is worried about giving proper food to their babies as they turn 6 months old and the same was for me and my wife. As we know that the right kind of food is essential for the overall growth and development of a baby.

I remember, when our daughter turned six, I was searching and browsing for the best food that we could give her. After deep research, I figured that millets could be the right food and started making recipes out of them.

In Southern India, in most houses, they start with millet porridge for their babies and they certainly know that it will keep their babies full for a longer time.

With millets, we can make a lot of recipes for babies but we started with millet porridge and khichdi. After taking millet food she gradually developed a taste for it. Today, after 7 years we are still following the journey and packing the food in her tiffin box made with millets.

You might have a question in your mind about when and how to start feeding millet to babies.

When a baby turns six, he/she can take millet. According to a study conducted by the National Institute of Nutrition, Hyderabad, a six-month baby can digest thick soft food. Thick food gives them more energy and nourishes them more than thin food. Millets can be introduced to babies with milk and slowly can make recipes with millet rice and dal in 2:1 proportion with ghee/oil. Gradually fresh vegetables can be added with millets.

In India, millet startups have come up with innovative millet-weaning products for toddlers and kids and these products have been accepted wholeheartedly by the mothers of India. Here, I will be sharing two inspiring stories of millet startups created by mothers.

Slurrp Farm, co-founders Shauravi Malik, and Meghana Narayan launched their millet startup in October 2016. They did the groundwork and invested time, energy, effort, and their hard saving money into extensive research and development for continuous 3 years. They understood what could be done differently by looking into the market.

Before coming to the millet business, both of them were super achievers in their respective fields. Shauravi, an alumni of St. Stephens and Cambridge University, worked for Sir Richard Branson's Group holding entity at Virgin Group and JP Morgan in London.
Meghana, a national-level swimmer, pursued her MBA from Harvard Business School and worked for McKinsey for seven years. They both were joined by a creative brain, Umang Bhattacharya who gave a distinct identity and brand to Slurrp Farm.

.

From the beginning, they could identify the gap in healthy eating options in the children's food market as they could not find high-quality foods for their own children. The products available were full of excess sugar, bad fats, and lots of preservatives and additives. It became a concern for them to bring products with zero junk and made with traditional organic ingredients.

It was not that easy. They followed a long process of trial and error, success and failure, and took on nutritionists, paediatricians, and industry specialists in developing their millet products. They tested their products with children and could figure out whether their products can run in the market.

Finally, the millet products came into the market with beautiful packaging using vibrant colors, characters, and storytelling which appealed to the children.
Now the products are available on their own website, e-commerce website, and over 800 stores in India and UAE.

The starting capital came from their own savings and the first angel funding came from their friends, family, and colleagues who believed in their ideas and products. They raised institutional funding of $2 million from Fireside Ventures and recently raised another $7 million in a fresh round led by the Investment Corporation of Dubai, the sovereign wealth fund of the Government of Dubai, and existing investor Fireside Ventures.

During the COVID-19 pandemic, the growth of Slurrp Farm accelerated to 10X as the consumers became more health conscious and this made investors invest more in this startup.

These two millet mompreneurs believe that healthy food need not come at the cost of taste, rather it should be fun, full of stories and colorful things children can enjoy with their food. Slurrp Farm is growing steadily with over Rs.50 crore of revenue run rate and aims to reach Rs.500 crore in revenue by 2025 enabling them to become the global Indian FMCG brand and this makes their vision of bringing back millets to the people in line with planet development goals.

Slurrp Farm, co-founders Shauravi Malik, and Meghana Narayan

A small message for you from these two millet mompreneurs is that the journey of building a brand and products is a long way. So, get yourself a partner for the trip and a group of good people who believe in your ideas and mission. No doubt a lot of challenges will come your way but working hard and keeping the customers at the center of your efforts will help.

Let's look at another inspiring story of a mother who had a strong passion to do impactful work before starting her millet startup and believed in giving Indian parents healthier options to feed their growing babies.

Shalini Santhosh started Early Foods in 2015 within the four walls of her home in Pune with a mission to provide fresh, organic and preservatives free food to children.

She grew up in a middle-class family in Bangalore where her parents believed in investing much in her education so that she could do impactful work in her life. She completed her engineering in Metallurgical and Material Sciences from NIT Trichy. She worked as a Business Consultant for ZS Associates, a global sales and marketing firm, and then she moved to other organizations where her work was strategizing and solving sales and marketing challenges which helped in her startup journey.

Shalini's dream is to create a visible impact. After becoming a mother, she decided to not return to a regular job. Instead, she wanted to become an entrepreneur. She started reading about successful startups, and their founders' journeys.

As soon as her son turned 6 months old, she introduced solid food but struggled to find the right wholesome healthy baby food. The products that were available in the market contained refined cereals, sugar, and preservatives.

She could find the gap in the products and thought of including sprouted ragi and other millet to make the weaning food and started her millet startup venture. In her product portfolio, she included porridge mixes, health drinks, cookies, and rusks for children.

From the beginning, she set up two principles in her startups. First, every product will be made using the traditional ingredients with 100% whole grain flour, cow-milk butter, dates, and jaggery for sweeteners, dry fruits and seeds, and a major portion of the super grain millet. The second principle was that all foods must be fresh and it must be packed only after getting the orders from the customers.

Early Foods products are available on her own online platform and other e-commerce websites like Amazon, Firstcry, BabyChakra, and BabyGogo and also on the shelves of organic stores in Mumbai, Bangalore, Delhi, Ahmedabad, and Surat. The products are also exported to the US. Most of the growth that happened was organic through word of mouth and social media.

Once a mother is satisfied and develops faith in the millet products, it gradually spreads very fast.

A message for you from Shalini, *"In the early years of a startup, you need to become single-handedly accountable for everything. With a small team, you need to manage every aspect of the business such as accounting, taxes, payments, procurement, quality assessment, and expansion, and should know what's happening all around as it's your brand and dream you need to carry forward".*

Nine

MILLET EXPORT BUSINESS - TAKING INDIAN MILLETS TO THE INTERNATIONAL MARKETS

The demand for millet is increasing, not only in the domestic market but also in the international markets. The demand for healthy food has increased during the current pandemic in India and globally. COVID-19 has given opportunities to promote millet and millet-based products.

It has been reported that there is an increase of 11.6% growth in the export of millets, exporting 79,459 metric tonnes in 2021 against 71,203 MT in the same period last year. This implies millet export from India is creating opportunities for entrepreneurs.

Today, we will understand the Status of Millets in India, Major importing countries, Support of Organizations in millet export, Initiatives of APEDA, Basic Requirements for Millet Export, Major interventions required in Millet Export from India, Some points for Millet Entrepreneurs looking for export and finally some success stories and some tools that will help you in understanding the millet business better.

Status of Millets in India:

As you know, India ranks first in terms of the production of millets. As per data from the Department of Agriculture and Farmers

Welfare, Government of India, India's production is about 173 lakhs metric tonnes which accounts for 80% of Asia and 20% of global production. India ranks 5th in Millet Export in the world.

Major Importing Countries:

The major export destinations of millet are Nepal, Saudi Arabia, Pakistan, UAE, Tunisia, Sri Lanka, Yemen Republic, Libya, Namibia, and Morocco. According to the report of the Directorate General of Commercial Intelligence and Statistics (DGCIS), in the year 2019-20, 0.08 million MT of millets was exported from India which was valued at 205.2 crores (28.75 million dollars).

Support of Organizations in Millet Export from India:

There are much-esteemed organizations in India supporting millet export. In the recent submission of the "White Paper on Millets" to Nitiyoag by the Indian Institute of Millet Research(IIMR), Hyderabad, it is well mentioned about the interventions and the stakeholders' role in millet export from India.

Sl. No.	Intervention	Description	Expected Outcomes	Stakehoders
1	Standards and Grades	Establishing the Standards and Grades for small millets, and also for the degree of polishing for transparent marketing	- Consumer safety - Increased processing units	FSSAI ICAR-IIMR CSIR-CFTRI IIT - Kharagpur
2	HS Codes	Establishing HS Codes for small millets for exporting	Increased Exports	APEDA ICAR-IIMR

3	Export demand Mapping	Identifying Export market trends and potential for various millet value-added products	Clear positioning strategies	ICAR-IIMR APEDA
4	Positioning Strategies	Framing the USPs for various product segments of domestic and international markets	Better penetration of products	ICAR-IIMR
5	Export Promotion Forum	Creation of Millet Export Promotion Forum with all concerned stakeholders for integrated export promotion nationally	-Strong sourcing linkages - Increased export traders, start-ups	ICAR-IIMR DAC and FW APEDA

Millet Export from India – Regulatory Measures and Export Strategies. Source: White Paper on Millets

Initiatives of APEDA in millet export from India:

The main motto of the Agricultural and Processed Food Products Export Development Authority (APEDA) is the export promotion of Agri products from the country and has the vision to establish India as a consistent supplier of quality and price-competitive products.

APEDA has come out with many promotional schemes for Export.

1. Export Infrastructure development schemes
2. Quality Development schemes
3. Market Development Schemes

Basic Requirement for Millet Export from India:

- Ability to export the quantity of product as required.
- Consistent supply
- Quality product
- Price competitive
- Meet the standard and grades of millets as per the importing countries' norms.

Advice to Entrepreneurs for Millet Export from India:

There is a huge export potential for millet value-added products. So, entrepreneurs should keep this in mind before starting startups.

- Develop innovative millet products.
- Develop products as per consumers' preferences and tastes.
- Technology development for superior quality products with enhanced shelf life.
- Focus on gluten-free products as the trend of gluten is increasing in western countries.
- Analyze the millet products in other countries and consumer preferences.

We can take the help of the Indian Institute of Millets Research, Hyderabad for developing value-added products from millet. This esteemed organization has supported many startups to develop innovative millet-based products.

Success Stories in Millet Export from India:

Recently organic Himalayan millets (Ragi and Barnyard Millet) have been exported from Uttarakhand to Denmark. In this journey, APEDA in collaboration with UKAPMB and Just Organik helped the millet farmers.

When we first started our venture in 2004, export was the only market available. However, as we looked more into the export business, we understood that in order to take advantage of the

potential, we need to have extremely good systems and processing infrastructure.
So, despite the fact that it was a difficult start, we were able to establish some fundamental processes and infrastructure in a few years. Exports will not be viable unless you first dominate the domestic market, said Dr.Rajashekar Reddy, Founder and MD, 24 Mantra.

Now, 24Mantra millet products are exported to international markets and have taken the space on the shelf of retail stores.

There is a range of millet products under the brand name Manna. It has done well in the domestic market as well as in the international markets. The millet products are exported to countries like the United Arab Emirates, Singapore, and many more. All these things were made possible by Murugan S, CEO, Southern Health Foods Private Limited.

Authentic Tools for Millet Export from India:
For the export of millet from India, you need to have all the documents like Registration of the firm, Bank Account Details, GST, PAN, and the Importer-Exporter Code (IEC) which is mandatory. Without the IEC number, no person can make an import or export that is granted by the Directorate General of Foreign Trade (DGFT). The nature of the firm obtaining IEC may be as "Proprietorship, Partnership, LLP, Limited Company, Trust, HUF, and Society."

To obtain the IEC number, you need to do registration in the DGFT portal (https://www.dgft.gov.in). It's very simple if you have all the documents ready in your hand. Visit the website and click on the "Apply for IEC". Just fill it up and you are done. Within a few days, you will get your IEC Code.

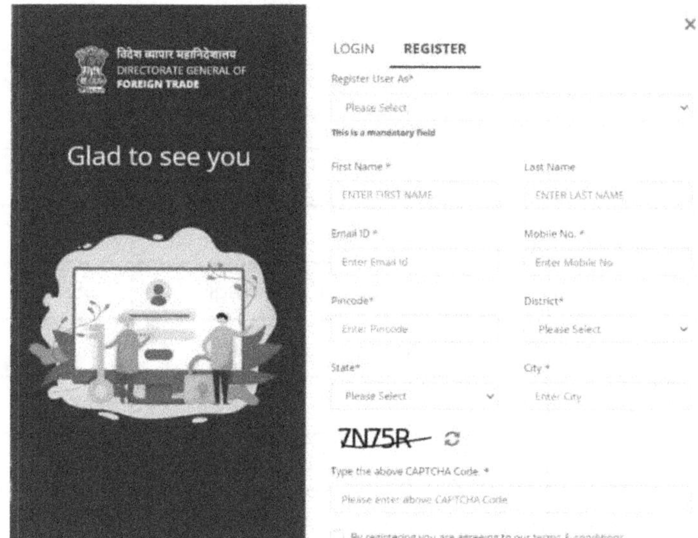

Registration for Import-Export Code

The next job is to know the HSN Code of the commodity that you are preparing to export. Here I will be showing how to know the HSN Code of millets. To find the code you need to visit the website of the Directorate General of Commercial Intelligence and Statistics (http://dgciskol.gov.in).

On the right side of the screen, you will find the “”8 Digit Commodity Classification”. Just click on it and this will take you to the Indian Trade Classification (Harmonized System)-2017 and you will find millets in Section -II under Vegetable products in chapter 10.

Heading No.	HS Code	ITC (HS)	Description	Units
			Grain Sorghum	
	100710	10071000	Seed	KGS

		10079000	Other	KGS
1008	100821		Millet Seed	
		10082110	Jawar	KGS
		10082120	Bajra	KGS
		10082130	Ragi	KGS
	100829		Other	
		10082910	Jawar	KGS
		10082920	Bajra	KGS
		10082930	Ragi	KGS

After getting the HS Code, now is the time to know the recent trends of millet export from India, which are the importing countries, the quantity of export, and value of the products. You may get a lot of data from private parties but to get authentic data without paying a single rupee is very important. So, let us look into the figures for 2021-22 and 2022-23 of Ragi. The HS Code of Ragi is "10082130".

After noting down the HS Code, visit the website of the Department of Commerce and Industry, Govt. of India (https://tradestat.commerce.gov.in) and click on the commodity-wise all countries under Exports and then select and put the value in Year, Commodity, Sort On, Value and submit. You will get all that you are looking for. I have done it for Ragi and the result is in front of you.

Department of Commerce
Export Import Data Bank
Export :: Commodity-wise all countries

Dated: 19/8/2022

Commodity: 10082130 RAGI Unit: KGS

S.No.	Country / Region	Values in Rs. Lacs			Quantity in thousands		
		[illegible]	[illegible]	[illegible]	[illegible]	[illegible]	[illegible]
1.	ANGOLA	0.01			0.02		
2.	AUSTRALIA	19.69	0.32		10.93	2.29	
3.	BAHARAIN IS	2.69	0.19		5.40	0.39	
4.	BELGIUM	0.43			0.54		
5.	BHUTAN	0.79	0.36		0.51	2.01	
6.	BRUNEI	0.50			1.23		
7.	CANADA	22.09	5.53		31.05	7.28	
8.	FIJI IS	0.01			0.01		
9.	FRANCE	0.19			0.37		
10.	GABON	0.01			5.00		
11.	GERMANY	0.65			0.86		

After knowing the trends, you have to know the global regulations and quality parameters of the importing countries and after getting the lead you need to further proceed with the certifications and documentation and make your products ready for export.

If you are very new to this import-export millet business, it is always advisable to start the trade within the country and then look for a third market (low-value market) like Bangladesh, Nepal, Bhutan, etc. Slowly understanding the dynamics of the business you can focus on the mid-value market and then the high-value market.
For export to the international market, you need to be very smart in every aspect.

- Packaging
- Delivery
- Shipment
- Certification
- Register with the plant quarantine.
- Identification of the market you want to enter.
- Consumer pattern of the importing country.
- Building a good product line
- Understanding the regulations and keeping the documentation in place.
- Infrastructure Certificate

India has made a significant improvement to the "Ease of Doing Business" by decreasing the number of mandatory paperwork needed for each import and export of commodities to three.

Following the DGFT's Notification, only three documents per export and import are necessary as two documents (Packing List and Commercial Invoice) required by Customs have been combined into one document, while RBI's Foreign Exchange Control Forms (SDF for exports and A-1 for imports) and the Ministry of Shipping's Terminal Handling Receipt (which were previously required) have been eliminated. The "Cargo Release Order" is a business document issued by the shipping line to the relevant importer and is not a mandatory document required by any regulatory body.

There is a huge potential for millet products in the international market. We need to capture it by doing proper strategies at the grassroots level and by market intelligence.

Ten

MILLET SOCIAL ENTREPRENEURSHIP - EMPOWERING WOMEN

EarthPoorna: Ensuring and supporting the livelihood of women and farmers

EarthPoorna, a social venture by Sucheta Bhandare of Pune involves women in the business and procures millet directly from farmers and thus ensures and supports the livelihood of women and farmers. It was a humble beginning with a passion for farming that attracted Sucheta to study the whole millet ecosystem and understand the problems faced by the women. She knew that women farmers face a lot of challenges apart from climate change, soil degradation, and crop loss but taking small steps led to the discovery of stark realities. To bring a small change in society, Sucheta started EarthPoorna.

"EarthPoorna" derives its name from mother earth. It has three contexts attached to it, one is the literal meaning which means 'full of Earth', the second one points towards something 'meaningful' from its Marathi root word and the third context is that which brings money to the homes of our Farmers.

Sucheta started with Finger Millet (Ragi) and slowly diversified her product portfolio taking millet as the main ingredient. From the beginning, she was aware of the health benefits of millet and this made her reach more people in India confidently.

It was interesting to listen to her journey from her childhood to starting this millet startup and creating a sensation among the people of India. Let us give ear to her amazing millet journey.

The short breaks at my school in Vadner used to be so interesting that even the thought of it makes me smile today. I used to take peanuts and jaggery, dates and grated coconut, roasted grams, and puffed rice on some days, and seasonal fruits, pulses, and healthy and nutritious ladoos on other days. During days-offs and holidays, my friends and I would go to the farms and happily devour whatever was growing there. Spending my childhood in a village in the district of Nashik meant that I had no other option for the junk food that kids in the cities eat today.

Today, although I live in a big city like Pune, my hunger pangs are still fulfilled by such simple preparation. All this was easily available to me back at home because my mother made it a point to put it in my Dabba(tiffin box). In cities, there are many out there who want to incorporate such a healthy diet into their lifestyle but have no time and sources to get hold of such products.

That is why we are bringing to you such preparations filled with love and health. A combination of your grandma's recipe and expert advice on diets suitable to our lifestyle is what you will find in our natural and tasty preparations. We at 'EarthPoorna Foods' are glad to serve you delicious food in your office, school, gym, college, and at your home.

The best thing about EarthPoorna is that the chemical-free raw materials are procured directly from the farmers. In the initial days, it was difficult to get ragi grains, but slowly Sucheta Bhandare convinced the farmers of her locality to cultivate and promised to pay a better price. Farmers were happy and started cultivating ragi in their fields when they could find a better market for their produce.

EarthPoorna has a team of dedicated and well-trained women who make delicious, healthy, and nutritious ragi ladoos. This venture brought about a change in the life of the women and improved their livelihood status.

EarthPoorna Ragi Ladoos impact the health of the consumers. Now, people have got a nice product to choose from. Ragi Ladoos has reached different corners of the country. The feedback from the consumers is amazing and they are recommending it to their friends and relatives. They liked the taste of the Ragi Ladoos. It is becoming a part of every festival in India. It has created positive vibes among consumers.

The Ragi Ladoos are made by maintaining proper hygiene and cleanliness. These products are tested in the Government Lab and a proper nutrients certificate is obtained and also certified by the *Food Safety and Standards Authority of India* (*FSSAI*). Ragi Ladoos are made under the guidance of a Nutritionist and Ayurveda practitioner.

Ragi Ladoos are made in four variants. The main ingredients of the ladoos are Ragi flour, Jaggery, Cow Ghee, dry fruits, dry dates, flax seed powder, and Cardamom powder. One of them is the multigrain ladoo which is made with a combination of pulses, flax seeds, jaggery, ghee, and almonds. Research has found that millet in combination with pulses improves the bioavailability and absorption of nutrients in the body.

This makes EarthPoorna's Ragi Ladoos unique in the market.

Making the ragi ladoos available on the online platform has increased the sales and could reach every corner in India. Adding Ragi Ladoos to your diet will definitely keep you and your family healthy. EarthPoorna's venture works for the sustainable development of farmers and simultaneously provides you with wholesome and healthy food. I hope this social enterprise will flourish more in the days to come and bring smiles to the face of the farmers and keep us healthy.

Millet Bank: Reviving Healthy and Nutritious Food Culture

Millet Bank is a social Millet Startup started on August 31st, 2020 with a mission to revive millet cultures by establishing market linkages between millet farmers, microentrepreneurs and consumers through a series of agroecological interventions. This initiative was founded by a Hyderabad-based entrepreneur, Vishala Reddy Vuyyala, who is a native of Mullur Krishnapuram, a village in the Chittoor district of Andhra Pradesh. She is a hospitality and tourism industry professional and has worked for 18 years in the tourism and hospitality development sectors. During the pandemic, she took the opportunity to move to her village but was shocked to see that her village farmers and relatives were suffering. The farmers were not having proper marketing opportunities and were not able to sell their products and make money.

That situation gave her a provoking thought to do something for the farmers and the idea of Millet Bank started. She was confident to use the marketing experiences that she learned through her professional career.

It was nice meeting Vishala on 18th, September 2021 and listening to her at an event ""Nutri-Cereals Multi-Stakeholder Mega Convention 3.0" held in Hyderabad. Millet Bank has the vision to boost farmers' income and quality of life by building a fair, sustainable, integrated, and inclusive value supply chain in the space of Millets. It is an initiative in taking the 7000 years old millet farming legacy forward to revive millet food cultures and nutritional diversity.

The logo of Millet Bank is inspired by "gadhe"- a space used to store grains. Its motto is the Sanskrit shloka "Lokah Samastah Sukhino Bhavantu" meaning may all beings everywhere be happy and free. Millet Bank is an end-to-end enterprise designed to 'Give back to the land what has been taken away. They are amalgamating multiple market linkages to benefit farmers, and entrepreneurs and create awareness among consumers. This has been done through a series of agro-ecological interventions such as Farmer Field Centers for farmers to sell their grains, an e-commerce platform for consumers to buy healthy and nutritious products and a collab center for micro-entrepreneurs related to millet and consumer engagement through sustainable gifting and social engagements.

In the beginning, it was not that easy as I faced many challenges. Convincing the farmers to change was a hard task as they dont see millets as profitable and thus they were reluctant to grow millets. But Vishala put her best efforts into training the farmers, connecting with the scientists and creating awareness about the native foods and culture, and meeting with the District Collector to discuss the plan of expanding the concept of Millet Bank.

It was also seen that the younger generations do not accept millet food and the idea of making value-added products came forward. Now they have developed a range of millet products like millet cookies and noodles in different variations. These millet products are easily available on their website, where consumers can buy them easily.

Millet Bank has set up a cultural gifting division, where the miniature of dolls associated with the culture and lifestyle of the farmers are collected from the local rural crafts. Vishala believes that agriculture is not just about food production but agriculture and farmers have a lot more responsibility towards their environment, families, and the most important the nation.

Millet Bank was the MABIF Incubatee and Vishala was awarded as one of the 'Best Women AgTech Entrepreneur' at the 4th edition of FICCI Agri Start-up Summit and Awards 2022.

Millet Bank is a great initiative promoting good food and a good lifestyle by engaging over 50 female farmers in the beginning and plans to engage more than 250 women. This has not just encouraged farmers to grow millet but also supports women farmers for better livelihood and empowers them to lead a happy life.

Eleven

ORGANIC AND NATURAL MILLETS

Organic and Natural millet are premium products that fetch better prices in the market. It has demand in the national and international markets. India's organic market is expected to exhibit a CAGR of 25.25%. Organic food gives consumers the assurance that it is free from pesticides and synthetic fertilizers.

The Government of India is promoting organic and natural farming by providing financial support to the farmers under Paramparagat Krishi Vikas Yojana(PKVY) and Bharatiya Prakritik Krishi Paddhati (BPKP).

Dr.Rajashekar Reddy, Founder, and MD, started the 24 Mantra 16 years back when there was not much awareness of organic food, and that too in a small market.
There were mainly two challenges: one was the building of a supply chain, where maintaining traceability was difficult. The other problems were in processing, packaging, and storage. There was no suitable technology and convincing farmers to do organic farming and educating consumers to eat organic food was difficult.

24 Mantra systematically tackled the supply chain and it took 7-8 years without using preservatives or chemicals. In terms of minor

millet, there was a challenge of getting the right seeds but in the case of major millet, there was no issue.
"For demand creation, the Government should run a program as "One Millet a Day Mission" , emphasized Dr.Rajashekar Reddy.

Initially, they started with their own store and invested in taking supermarket shelf space. They had to do similar things for millet by putting a shelf and a person educating consumers about millet.

"If you are self-funded, the ability to invest becomes very difficult. So, early in our life, we realized that with our own funding we will never be able to move higher in retail. So we convinced some of the institutional investors to invest. They looked at the size of the market opportunity and our ability to convert that opportunity into a reality. So we were able to secure a large number of findings," said Dr.Reddy.

If we are able to convince 10% of people to have millet once a day, we are talking about a 30-40 million dollar opportunity. The grocery market is about 600 million dollars. So, there is a huge opportunity pointed out by Dr. Rajashekar Reddy.

He added, "Unless you conquer the domestic market, exports will not be a viable kind of approach. "You have to win at home to win outside". 40 years back rice was a luxury for most of the south Indian people but today eating millet has become a luxury. Millets are more expensive than rice and wheat. So, changing food habits is not going to be easy".

Organic and Natural millets have huge potential in the future. It is the right time to promote and do business in this organic millet industry.

Twelve

MILLET RECIPES - TEACHING HOW TO COOK MILLET PERFECTLY

When it comes to millet recipes, people still face difficulty. But if we know the proper way and techniques to cook millet, it becomes easy. The removal of anti-nutritional compounds from the millet is a mandatory requirement prior to its consumption otherwise it can create serious health hazards. From ancient times, different techniques and treatments have been given to millet grains at the household level to make them suitable for human consumption. They include soaking, heating, roasting, fermentation, cooking, etc

The right technique to cook millet is to go with measurement. If the measurement of millet grains and water is perfect, we get the right cooked millets. Let us follow some tips before and after cooking millet.

Soaking of Millet:

When both parents are working, there is always a hurry in cooking breakfast or lunch. So, we decide what to cook the next day before going to bed. We always soak the millet overnight and it becomes easy and fast to cook. The best thing is that soaking millet for 6-8 hours breaks down the phytic acid and it becomes easy to digest. If you are planning to cook millet, remember to soak it overnight.

Measurement of Water and Grains:

We require water as per the Millet Recipe we plan to cook. Let me give you the exact measurement for different millet recipes.
Millet Rice – 1:2 (Millet: Water)
Millet Upma with Vegetables – 1:2.5
Millet Khichdi with Pulses and Vegetables – 1:3
Millet Pongal/Porridge – 1:4 (Millet: Water)

Cooking Time:
Generally, millet requires about 20-25 minutes for cooking. If you are cooking in a pressure cooker, you need to go for 2 whistles on a medium flame, and if in an earthen pot/vessel you need to cook for 12-13 minutes on medium flame by covering the pot with a lid. After 12-13 minutes turn off the gas and give a resting time of 10 minutes. Resting time makes the millet fluffy.
When you are cooking in a pressure cooker for up to 2 whistles, you need to allow it to rest for 10 minutes or so to release pressure.

I see a lot of opportunities in teaching people how to cook millet and start the millet journey. Nowadays you can find lots of videos and blogs on the internet about millet recipes. You must be thinking about how teaching cooking with millet can be a millet startup. Let me introduce someone who does a workshop on Cooking with millet and she has been connected to people from more than 36 countries.

Shalini Rajani, founder of Crazy Kadchi and a Millet Coach, holds an innovative millet cooking workshop for all groups. She has been conducting millet workshops for more than 8 years. Started her journey with healthy food and healthy cooking but she could find people suffering from gluten tolerance and people started moving towards vegan foods. There were incidents where more people were suffering from diabetes even kids were facing the problem of diabetes. Understanding millet in a better way, she realized that Millet is the future, especially in the world of culinary.

Shalini did her B.Sc(Hons) in Chemistry and after graduation, she has done a course on multimedia. Then joined Journalism in Mass Communication at Aligarh Muslim University and was the gold medalist. After post-graduation landed in Advertising and worked as a Copywriter. She left the job when she was a Copy Supervisor.

Shalini was always into cooking and experimenting with foods and then she realized that she might be a writer by profession but a Chef by heart. Although she does not possess any culinary degree but participated in the Master Chef India season-4 in 2012. In this competition, she cleared a few rounds and from there she decided to take her journey further. It was at that stage of her life where she used all the learnings, skills, and knowledge she gained from B.Sc(Chemistry), Multimedia, Advertising, and Communication in her Millet Journey Workshop.

Previously she was conducting the workshop in offline mode and during the COVID pandemic; she started a 6 weeks Millet Journey and then moved to 10 weeks. In her workshop, she brings the millet grains in an interesting way so that people do not think of it as sick people's food.

In her workshop she teaches the basics of millet grains, making the participants understand the different types of millets and the importance of millet in a very systematic way. During the 10 weeks journey, she teaches how to soak millet, make millet flour at home, millet rice, biriyani, noodles, pasta, rusks, cakes, biscuits, cookies, different types of bread, millet salads, and many more. In addition to that, she conducts one-to-one sessions to understand the participant's health problems if any, guides them accordingly, and also shares pre-recorded unedited videos. She also gives a complimentary session on gut health, and shares how to make an ambali recipe interesting, sourdough starter, baking with millet, and provides recipe booklets.

She shares with her participants that removing phytates, oxalates, and other anti-nutrients from millet is a very important step and this can be done by properly washing and soaking. She believes that millet is for everyone and healing with millet is possible but people need to understand the technique of bringing millet into the regular diet.

In 2021 Shalini took her Millet Journey workshop to 24 countries and 46 cities across the globe. She simply says "Millets are Fun". In addition to her workshop, she writes for ""The Indian Express"" where she shares interesting Millet recipes.

Thirteen

MILLET BEVERAGES INDUSTRY - BOOMING IN THE FUTURE

Even today, when I go to the tribal areas of Odisha, I find people making beverages with millet and that too with Finger Millet and it is commonly known as *Landha*. They follow the simple process of soaking, germination, grinding, cooking, and finally fermentation.
North Eastern states have many millet traditional beverages. In Sikkim, you can find Chhang, commonly known as Tongba. The whole millet is cooked and then fermented to make the beverage.

Cereals of all types are used as the base for fermented dishes and drinks. Even in Africa cereal grains including sorghum (Sorghum bicolor (L.) Moench), millets (pearl and finger millets [Pennisetum glaucum (L.) and Eleusine coracana]), and maize [Zea mays (L.)] are used as raw materials to make various types of food and beverages.

There are two categories of drinks: alcoholic and nonalcoholic. The majority of the time, microorganisms including yeast, lactic acid bacteria, and acetic acid bacteria are used in the fermentation process to create millet drinks. The primary ingredients in these beverages that increase the amylolytic enzymes for starch decomposition are dry malt and germinated millet.

In Nigeria, it was discovered that using malted sorghum grains as a source of fermentable sugars was favorable. Sorghum cultivars, including SK 5912, Farafara, and HQSV grains, are also used for malting. Of which the HQSV variety was discovered to be the best variety for malting. Sorghum malting, often known as African "Bantu" beer, is a traditional process in South Africa.

Rabadi is one of the most well-known and traditional non-alcoholic drinks. It is prepared by fermenting pearl millet flour with butter milk. It is a traditional popular beverage in the North-Western states of India.

The first brewery to use nutri-cereals in beer jugs is Bengaluru's Toit Brewery and they have come up with great handcrafted beers. This will result in a decrease in the import of barley malt from other countries.

Let me share the journey of a young budding entrepreneur from Semiliguda, Odisha who has taken the idea from the grass root level and taken a step to start his millet startup H2M Food and Beverages Pvt Ltd and, H2M Dhono Foundation in collaboration with 1200 millet farmers.

Santosh Kumar Khemundu along with Deepak Singh and K Govinda Raju Nagabhushan came up with an idea of giving people a plant-based drink with a mission to take the Ragi-based drinks to the urban consumers. They believe that ragi-based drinks keep people fit and strong. They have seen it in young and old men of Koraput who take ragi-based drinks (*Mandia Pejo*) everyday.

They experimented and infused traditional drinks with chocolate, vanilla, and fresh fruit flavors to give them a contemporary twist. They have already sold more than 5000 glasses of drink in different exhibitions and other platforms in just six months.

They diversified to the confectionery segment and are also producing baked goods like cookies, and cupcakes in modern flavors with their own R&D team. It took them a year to extract the best out of millet. They believe in eliminating maida from their foods. Upon receiving good response and feedback from the consumers, it gave them encouragement and inspiration to make big plans and stand tall to make H2M brand known for Health to Mankind.

They have been incubated with KIIT Technology Business Incubator (KIIT TBI). And after a few months, they were offered funding of Rs. 2 crores from a Singapore-based private equity firm. It was followed up by multiple investment opportunities from private investors as well as the state and central government. These findings will take them to find more opportunities in the millet-based food and beverages industry.

They have plan to manufacture their products in Koraput itself as they think this will provide employment to the youths, motivate farmers to grow millet, and assure them of a good price for their millet produce.

In this millet startup journey, they have been associated with many groups and incubators. In 2017, they bagged a NIDHI-EIR (Entrepreneur in Residence) fellowship from the Department of Science and Technology, Government of India, worth Rs.3 lakh for one year. In 2018, they got listed as one of the top startups in Startup India-Odisha Yatra and were awarded Rs.50,000. They bagged the first position in a business plan competition called Sociovation 3.0 and were awarded a cash prize of Rs.50,000. They were also felicitated by the ambassador of the Netherlands to India for being one of the top five startups in the Green Business Challenge, held at New Delhi. In the same year, they bagged seed funding of Rs. 20 lakh from Villgro Social Entrepreneur Incubator and started their real journey as a startup. In 2019, they also received a fellowship and grant of a combined Rs.20 lakh for a year from Startup Odisha for being one of the best startups in the Startup India-Odisha Yatra.

In 2020, they were funded under the N-GRAIN grant under the Rashtriya Krishi Vikas Yojana(RKVY) by the Ministry of Agriculture, Government of India. In 2021, they were selected by the Ministry of Social Justice for Venture Capital Fund. Finally, after collaborating with more than 1200 farmers, they received MSME grant funding of Rs.5 crore for a millet processing unit, and progress is in full swing in helping the millet farmers of Koraput, Odisha. Recently in the year 2022, they were shortlisted in Startup India Innovation Week as one of the top agri-based startups.

Finally upon asking Santosh Kumar Khemundu, "What is their dream?". He responded, "Their dream is to make Koraput an Agri-manufacturing hub."

PART- IV
GROWING MILLET BUSINESS DIGITALLY

One

MILLET BRAND BUILDING

Brand building is a process to boost brand awareness, promote a specific product, establish connections and provide value to the target audience through campaigns. In the Millet industry, it is very much essential to make awareness among the consumers using proper promoting techniques and campaigns so that it can create an image in the marketplace.

The largest consumer survey ever undertaken was conducted by ICRISAT about the consumer insights on millet, interviewing 15,522 people from 7 major cities in 7 states of South, West, North, and Eastern India: Ahmedabad, Bengaluru, Chennai, Delhi, Hyderabad, Kolkata, and Mumbai. When people were asked about their main source of health and food information, about 85% of people listed Social Media(51%) and Friends/Family(34%). Social media was the largest source of information and that shows social media is indispensable to the efforts to reach consumers.

The main motive for bringing this chapter to you is to understand the concepts of brand building, the methods, the tools for brand building, and an overview of the analytics in millets. The brand can be built through a website, online advertising, content publishing, sales, and customer service. But it is important to determine your brand's purpose and how you differentiate from others, what problems you can solve and why should people care about your brand.

Concepts of Brand Building and Methods:

You should always focus on the goal that differentiates from the competition and persuade a consumer to buy from you over them. It can be done by properly analyzing your competitors. So, competitor analysis should be done by collecting all the information on the competitors' products and services, going through the reviews on social media, and their presence in online and offline markets.

The best tool that you can use to know about the millet products available in India and the International market is "Millet Finder". It is an interactive map that allows you to look for companies that produce millet and sorghum products.

"Millet Finder" was launched at Food Tech Expo on 25th, November 2020 by the International Crops Research Institute of the Semi-Arid Tropics (ICRISAT) and ICAR-Indian Institute of Millets Research, Hyderabad. It helps users in finding 500 millet products across 30 countries. Millet products are categorized based on Country, Crops, and Type (Baby Food, Baking, Beverages, Flakes, Flour, Grains, Multi grains, Pasta, Ready to Eat, and Ready to Cook).

Millet Finder gives an idea about the millet products available in a particular country. It helps users to know about the consumers' tastes, target the untapped millet markets, and to know the nutritional value of the millet products. It also helps in knowing the consumer demand in a particular place; it brings awareness about millet products for a consumer, and finally helps new millet entrepreneurs to reach customers.

Before building a brand you must work on your target audience more precisely and your key message for them. For example, to promote millet-weaning food for babies, your target consumer is moms, who make the decision in selecting the baby food. You can say that the right food without preservatives with a richness of nutrients.

After targeting the audience, it's time to understand the consumer persona like age, gender, place, income, and education level. This will help you in properly placing your ads and reaching the right consumers.

Marketing Tools for Brand Building:

Selecting the right kind of marketing tools for brand building is very important to promote your products and services to the clients. There are many tools in the market, but we will discuss the major right tools.

- Website
- SEO and content promotion
- Social Media Promotion
- Email Promotion
- Paid Advertising
- Analytics

Website: A website is an important promotion tool for business growth and brand building. This is the place where you can make your users connect with you in the long run by giving them a better experience.

But before building and launching your website, you must have all the correct information and your complete story to tell to your customers. There are 5 questions to be asked before launching the website and making it available for the users.

- Value - Does your content/products/services will make their valuable time spent on your website worthwhile?
- Usefulness - Does your website satisfy users' requirements?
- Findable - Is your website easily navigable?
- Usability - Is your website easy to use and mobile-friendly?
- Credibility - Does your brand, identity, content, services, and products build trust and belief in the user?

I think when all the answers to the above questions satisfy you, then it's the right time to launch your website.

SEO and Content Promotion: Right content and doing SEO (Search Engine Optimization) properly will generate relevant organic traffic to your website and thus improve the brand image and create more awareness. As you know, valuable content is the most effective way to build organic traffic and that will satisfy the visitor's intent. So, a well-defined content-promoting strategy can help you in connecting with the right audience and support them through their consumer journey, building trust to ultimately lead to conversions. And conversions over time build enough knowledge to create a community around it.

It is very important to start publishing content on millet, generating traffic, and building a community as early as possible. Most millet startups wait for the product to be ready before they think of creating a buzz in the market. Content is the most cost-effective as you are targeting the perfect consumers.

For building the right content you need to focus on the following points:

- Maintaining a diary and writing which content can resonate with your target audience?
- Frequency and the time of publishing your content.
- Arranging the content in a proper way.
- How can the content be found in the organic search results and that too on the first page of the Google search.

Suppose, you are targeting people suffering from diabetes and as you know millet is good for diabetes. You need to take your millet products to the right people and convince them that your product is the best for controlling diabetes. You can do so by writing the best content on "best millets for diabetes" so that the content appears on the first page of the Google search and it will be better if it ranks on the top. When it appears on the top, the number of visitors to your website will increase and ultimately lead to conversions.

To give you some glimpse of the content that I have built on millet, let's type "Best Millets for Diabetes" in Google Search. You can find my content at the top.

best millets for diabetes

All · Shopping · Images · Videos · News · More · Tools

About 2,42,000 results (0.40 seconds)

https://milletadvisor.com › millets-for-diabetes

5 Best Millets for Diabetes that lowers blood sugar

15-Jan-2022 — Types of **Millets for Diabetes**: · 1. Barnyard **Millet**, 65.6, 13.6, 4.82 · 2. Browntop **Millet**, 61.37, 12.5, 4.90 · 3. Foxtail **Millet**, 60.2, 6.7, 8.98.

Millets for Diabetes · Types of Millets for Diabetes · Recipes with Millets for Diabetes

In this way, you can build your content around your millet products and keep engaging your consumers and in the long run, this will help in creating a brand in the market.

Social Media Promotion:

As per the large-scale survey report on ""Accessing Millets and Sorghum Consumption Behavior in Urban India"", it has been found that the source of information on health and foods is Social media which is the most influential, about 50.7% of the respondents reported Social Media is the main source.

So, Social Media is one of the best platforms to educate, communicate and interact with consumers. To make social media more engaging you need to publish original and relevant content and build community.

Following better media strategies will help you to achieve and increase connections with your community. These all cannot happen in one or two days rather you need to post content consistently across all the social media networks that you handle. Once your end consumers start building trust, then you can advocate your millet products. So, selecting the correct social media networks will help you in growing your millet business.

Let us see the most common social media networks that are helping in brand building and what are the regular actions to be taken.

- **Facebook:** Facebook is the platform where people spend time engaging with their friends and family members and sometimes while scrolling they stop on the post that catches their eye and subsequently grabs their attention. So, posting on Facebook at least once every day with photographs or graphics will generate a lot of interaction.

- **LinkedIn:** It has been observed that most of the users navigate to the company's website from LinkedIn more than any other social media network. Posting at least 4-5 times per week with relevant content on millets will drive organic traffic to your website and subsequently increase the engagement of the visitors. Moreover, LinkedIn looks more professional and the chances of collaboration and connections will increase. Setting up branded company pages and publishing long-form content is a great way to reach an engaged audience and build your company's brand. The more long-form posts you publish, the more credibility you will build and the stronger your millet brand will become. Building a brand on LinkedIn will increase the chances of being discovered and bring more opportunities as well for your company.

- **Youtube:** Youtube is a great platform for creating brand awareness. You may have observed that good brands are not just trying to connect with new users and make a sale the right way but they create brand awareness by showcasing what they do and what they have to offer.
  In today's scenario, users like to watch content rather than create it and even respond to the content. If you want to engage in brand building, create content that your targeted audience is looking for. Let's suppose your audience is looking for millet recipes, you can start with

a keyword search and can find out how many search volumes are there per month.

You can know by using a tool like keywordtool.io. In this way, you can search for other keywords in the millet sector. After knowing the search volume, you can start making videos by offering unique content that really resonates with your targeted audience. As you know stories are powerful and simply telling the story of how and why your brand was created, will enhance the engagement rate.

- **Twitter:** Twitter is a great tool to build your millet brand and spread awareness about your millet business. Here are the ways for building a brand on Twitter.
    - Use your brand name for building a brand on Twitter.
    - Use your brand logo as your Twitter picture.
    - Send tweets that provide useful information on millets to customers. You can add a link to more information on your company's website.
    - Send tweets to new blog posts or videos you have created.
    - Ideally, you should tweet 10-20 times a day.
    - Use one or two hashtags to broaden your targeted audience and gain additional followers.

Email Promotion:

Email promotion or marketing is the best tool where you can get the highest click rate from your targeted audience. So, it is very important to build an email list for brand building as well as promotion of your products. Once you build the list, it becomes easy for you to broadcast your message with just a few clicks. You can build the subscribers list through opt-in-forms on your website. You can customize your forms as per your need. There are different forms to execute on your website.

- Pop-ups
- Sidebars
- Scroll mats

- Slide-ins
- Lead magnet forms
- Landing page forms

Once you have set up your forms the next important thing is to tag your subscribers as per your campaigns. You can use different kinds of email campaigns to target your audiences.

- Newsletter Subscription
- New product pre-booking
- Non-promotional blogs
- Product Offer Campaigns

Email promotion helps you to drive traffic to your website and increases conversions. Nowadays there are many email marketing tools available in the market and the best thing I prefer to do with this tool is automation. Automation saves your time and energy in managing your subscribers and delivering the right content to the right person without any errors.

Analytics:

It is very important to keep a watch on the progress of your promotion in brand building. Monitoring the progress weekly, monthly, and year-over-year will help you to understand which promotion activities are giving the highest output. It is seen that most small businesses don't use analytics tools to trace their performance. If you have built up your website, then you can use Google Analytics. It can provide you with lots of information regarding real-time data, audience behavior, content reach, top referrals, top social media traffic, top keywords, traffic sources, locations, and many more.

Paid Advertising:

Building a brand or promoting a product can happen with paid advertising. With the increase of opportunities and competitive market, it becomes very difficult to solely rely on organic channels to deliver traffic. It is very important to understand how paid advertising works and how best to benefit from it to achieve your business goals. Basically paid advertising is an online advertising model where advertisers bid to participate in order to show their ads. Ads come in many formats and shapes like text, images, banners, videos, etc.

There are many online advertising channels like Google Ads, Facebook Ads, Twitter Ads, LinkedIn ads, Quora Ads, and many more. Advertising platforms give you access to a lot of information about your audiences and this data can help you to understand your audience in a better way.

Millet brand building is an integral part of millet startups' business development. You must always keep in mind to understand the preferences and demands of your consumers. You know putting consistent effort will increase your brand presence and make your millet startup successful.

PART - V

SUPPORT TO START MILLET STARTUPS

One

INSTITUTIONAL SUPPORT IN INDIA

Nutrihub (https://www.nutrihubiimr.com), is a technology business incubator (TBI) established in 2017 hosted by ICAR- Indian Institute of Millets Research (IIMR), Hyderabad and funded by the Department of Science and Technology (DST) and RKVY-RAFTAR for identifying, nurturing and promoting Nutri-cereals startups across the country by vetting ideas from early stage entrepreneurs and startups.

Nutrihub is one of the largest Technology incubators in India. It provides last-mile connectivity with consumers and necessitates demand generation. It leverages technology generation from the Centre of Excellence on Millets, IIMR to commercialize.

Nutrihub beyond this handholding of startups also offers the infrastructure for the production of value-added products as a startup facility and mentoring, Research and Development (R & D) support, training, market facilitation, and industry and government market connectivity.

Nutrihub-TBI facilitates funding support for startups and entrepreneurs through two giant-in-aid programs of RKVY-RAFTAAR. One is the N-GRAIN (Seed Support Funding) program that provides grants of up to Rs.25 lakhs for early-stage start-ups with a minimum viable product in the market.

The other program is NEST (Agri Entrepreneurship program) which provides grants up to Rs.5 lakhs. To date, IIMR's Nutrihub has incubated 175+ startups facilitating grants to the tune of Rs.3.42 crores to at least 40 startups.

Incubation Program:

The Incubation Program is designed to help start-ups grow in a streamlined fashion by setting up the work plan and business goals during the course of incubation and assessing the progress of the goals on a month-on-month basis until they graduate/exit the incubation facility. The start-up will be assessed on a continual basis to ensure the progress is maintained and a relevant support system is provided or work is done towards making it accessible.

Duration of the Program: 12 Months.

All the incubatees undergoing the Nutrihub Incubation Program will go through a structured program and will have access to the below offerings during the course of the Incubation program:

- Plug and Play Dedicated Space at Nutrihub Incubator with ready-to-use office infrastructure.
- Structured Program support with monthly tracking of progress.

- Connection with Nutri Hub Network and Partners
- Service Providers
- Mentors and Experts
- Investors and Financial Institutions
- Industry and Academic Bodies
- Assistance with business and technical knowledge as a part of the program.
- Free/Discounted Access to Start-up Events and Training at the local/ national level by Nutrihub and its partners as applicable.
- Promotion of your start-up to visitors at IIMR, showcase on the incubator website, and any official

communications/ events conducted by Nutri Hub as applicable.

- Paid Access to Nutrihub Labs and Manufacturing/ Production Facilities
- Access to start-up resources, information, and communications on agribusiness activities, events, opportunities, and networking avenues at national-level Agri-exhibitions and entrepreneurship melas.
- Access to Freebies/ Discounts/ Deals that Nutrihub strikes partnerships on to benefit the incubatee start-ups.
- Nutrihub meeting rooms (Based on fair usage policies).
- Nutrihub Cafeteria and Canteen (on availability)

Some of the notable millet startups incubated under Nutrihub-IIMR incubation programmes are performing well in the industry.

1. InnerBeing
2. Health Sutra
3. Millet Chef
4. Bliss Tree
5. Slurrp Farm
6. Millet Amma
7. Green Tatwa
8. Grami Foods
9. Sudhanya
10. Doctor Millets

National Institute of Food Technology, Entrepreneurship, and Management (NIFTEM), Thanjavur (An Institute of National Importance, formerly Indian Institute of Food Processing Technology- IIFPT) provides support to the millet entrepreneurs in technology transfer and developing innovative millet products.

Centre for Innovation and Agripreneurship (CIA):
It is hosted at the National Institute of Agricultural Extension Management (MANAGE). It provides a one-stop solution for creating successful ventures in

agriculture and allied sectors. Our Agri Innovation Launchpad will empower people to fulfill their dreams and create the next big thing in the agricultural sector for aspiring enthusiasts and entrepreneurs.

CIA navigates innovation from Ideation to full-scale commercialization, with our unique methodology, which gives a robust ecosystem from discovering ideas to delivering high-value propositions in a sustainable environment.

The center's main focus is to promote the development of innovative products for Startups, which cater to the most disruptive problems in the agricultural sector. It aims at creating more employment opportunities and wealth creation, thus adding to the inclusive growth of the country's GDP.

The CIA nurtured the Agricultural Community with high-value Capacity Building programs that trained about 72,136 professionals, out of which 28,757 have set up their enterprises. The center aims at taking these agripreneurs to the next level by creating high-impact ventures through the incubation center.

Council of Scientific and Industrial Research (CSIR)-Central Food Technological Research Institute, Government of India, Mysuru. **CSIR-CFTRI** has developed many technologies based on millets and a large number of these have been successfully transferred to small and Medium Enterprises.

Two

STATE AND CENTRAL GOVERNMENT SCHEMES FOR MILLET STARTUPS

1. **Production Linked Incentive scheme for Food Processing Industry (PLISFPI):**

The main objective of this scheme is to support the creation of global food manufacturing champions; promote Indian brands of food products; increase employment opportunities for off-farm jobs, and ensure remunerative prices of farm produce and higher income to farmers.

Incentivizing manufacturing of four major food product segments i.e. Ready to Cook/ Ready to Eat (RTC/RTE) including millet-based foods, processed fruits and vegetables, marine products, and Mozzarella Cheese.

Support for branding and marketing abroad to incentivize the emergence of strong Indian brands.

2. **Pradhan Mantri Formalization of Micro Food Processing Enterprises (PMFME):**

This scheme was launched under the Atmanirbhar Bharat Abhiyan and is currently implemented in 35 states and Union Territories (UTs).

- The scheme is to enhance the competitiveness of existing individual micro-enterprises in the unorganized segment of the food processing industry and promote formalization of the sector and support Farmer Producer Organizations (FPOs), Self Help Groups (SHGs), and Producers Cooperatives along their entire value chain.

- It aims at providing increased access to common services like common processing facilities, laboratories, storage, packaging, marketing, and incubation services.

- Integration with an organized supply chain by strengthening branding and marketing and supporting the transition of existing 2, 00,000 enterprises into a formal framework.

- The scheme adopts the One District One Product (ODOP) approach to reap the benefits of scale in terms of procurement of inputs, availing common services, and marketing of products. There may be more than one cluster of ODOP products in one district. There may be clusters of ODOP products consisting of more than one adjacent district in a state. The states would identify the food product for a district, keeping in perspective the focus of the scheme on perishables.

Millets as part of ODOP Scheme:

1. Malkangiri and Nuapada (Odisha)
2. Tirap (Arunachal Pradesh)
3. Komaram Bheem and Mahabubnagar (Telangana)
4. Dharmapuri, Virudhunagar (Tamil Nadu)
5. Nandurbar, Solapur, Thane (Maharashtra)
6. Davanagere (Karnataka)
7. Poonch (Jammu and Kashmir)
8. Dang (Gujarat)
9. Sukma (Chattisgarh)

Three

CENTRAL GOVERNMENT AND STATE MILLET MISSIONS

The Government of India and the State Government have realized the importance of millets in building nutritional security and come up with new initiatives to promote millets in the country. The international year of millets 2023 has made the mandate to scale up the interventions for increasing the millet area and production and diversifying the processing machinery and technologies to cater millet domestic market and export markets. In the past decade, millets have made placed in different policy papers and subsequent efforts were made to revive the millets again in the food chain.

The following are some of the important Initiatives, Millet missions, and Schemes undertaken in India to promote millet production, processing, and value addition.

1. Initiative for Nutritional Security through Intensive Millets Promotion (INSIMP) was launched in the year 2012 under Rashtriya Krishi Vikas Yojana (RKVY), where Rs.300 crore was allocated to advancing equipment and technology. In this scheme demonstrations of improved packages and practices were conducted along with the post-harvest technologies. Processing and value-

addition techniques were undertaken to generate consumer demand for millet-based food products.

In the selected districts, technology demonstrations were organized in compact blocks for four categories of millets, i.e. Sorghum, Pearl Millet, Finger Millet, and Small Millets.

To promote new varieties/hybrids in millets, farmers were supported by providing incentives of Rs.3000/quintal for hybrid seeds and Rs.1000/quintal for high-yielding varieties(HYVs) of which 75% incentives were directly passed to the farmers and 25% for handling and processing charges.

National demonstrations cum training centers were planned to be set up at the Indian Institute of Millets Research (IIMR) for Sorghum (Previously known as Directorate of Sorghum Research (DSR), University of Agriculture Sciences (UAS), Bengaluru for Finger Millet and Small Millets and Chaudhary Charan Singh (CCS) Hisar Agriculture University, Hisar for Pearl Millet. These Institutions were entitled to provide entrepreneurship development and training and facilitate market linkages.

Demonstration-cum-training unit was planned to be set up in selected 100 Krishi Vigyan Kendras(KVK). A single complete post-harvest processing unit (3-in-one destoner cum grader cum cleaner + Pearling machine) and Secondary processing unit (Rava/Flaking machine-Jowar, Popping Roaster- Ragi, Parboiling - Pearl Millet) were installed at the total cost of Rs.4 lakhs.

Odisha Millet Mission:

Special Programme for Promotion of Millets in Tribal Areas of Odisha is one of the unique projects in the agriculture department which focuses on improved production of Nutri-cereals, local consumption, procurement under MSP, and distribution through PDS. The mission is initiated in the financial year 2017-18. The mission has been successfully implemented in 84 blocks and 15 districts and from 2022-23 it is extended to 142 blocks in 19 districts for implementation.

The program started working in 7 districts with 8,030 farmers and in the span of 5 years it has scaled up to 15 districts with 1,17,000 farmers.

Objectives of the Odisha Millet Mission:

1. Increasing household consumption of millets by 25% to the baseline.
2. Revalorization of millet food cultures in urban and rural areas.
3. Conservation and promotion of millet landraces through seed system of landraces
4. Promotion of post-harvest and primary processing enterprises on millets.
5. Improving productivity of millet-based crop system systems
6. Promotion of millet value-addition enterprises in rural and urban areas of Odisha
7. Inclusion of millets in PDS, ICDS, MDM, Welfare Hostels, and others.
8. Facilitating the millet markets and exports of millet-based products from Odisha

Highlights of activities carried out under the Odisha Millets Mission

- The program is implemented with support from 61 NGOs as facilitating agencies and 84 Community-Based Organizations as implementing agencies in 84 Blocks of 15 Districts. The program is expanded and extended to 142 blocks in 2022-23.
- Last year 52,800 Ha areas was covered under improved agronomic practices under diversified millets with 1.17 lakh farmers and incentivized for the adoption of improved agronomic practices. Planned for 81700

hectares of Millet Crop for 2022-23 with 1.5 Lakh farmers.

- The Govt of Odisha had procured a sum of 323019.05 quintals of Ragi from 41286 farmers during the KMS-2021-22 at an MSP of Rs.3377 per quintal of Ragi. Planned for 6 Lakh quintals Ragi to be procured during 2022-23 from farmers at Minimum Support Price.
- A total of 169 Community Managed Seed Centres are established by the WSHGs and FPOs to conserve local landraces and provide quality seeds timely. 227 Custom hiring centers established by WSHGs and FPOs to provide farm equipment to farmers at a minimal hiring cost.
- A total of 578 Ragi Thresher units have been established through WSHGs/FPOs in order to reduce the drudgery involved in the threshing of Ragi. A total of 20 nos. of Ragi Cleaner-Cum-Grader have been established through WSHGs/FPOs under Odisha Millets Mission. A total of 287 nos. of Pulverizer units have been set up through WSHGs/FPOs.
- A total of 96 nos. of Millets-Based Tiffin Centers and 2 no. of Quick Service Restaurants and Millets Shakti Outlets were established respectively in urban and rural areas to raise the year-round demands of millets.
- Under PDS @2 kg of Ragi per ration cardholder has been supplied to 50 lakh Ration Card Beneficiaries for one month in 14 districts as a substitute of rice from the quantity procured during KMS 2019-20.
- Inclusion of Ragi Laddu in Keonjhar and Sundargarh covering more than 1.5 lakh children.

FPOs in Odisha Millet Mission:

- **Farmer Producer Organization (FPO)** - 75 Farmer Producer Organizations (FPO) are promoted and registered with the objective of the FPO is working on the promotion of farmer collective, developing, and sustaining business models, access to credit, input supply to farmers, farm advisory.

- 23 FPOs were registered with NeML, 10 FPOs are registered with APEDA as export agencies, and 14 are registered with Reliance retail for marketing of millets.
- 17716 female and 12420 male farmers are associated with 75 FPO as shareholders and members. 16 FPOs were empaneled as block procurement agencies during KMS 2020-21 and currently during KMS 2021-22, 56 FPOs are empaneled. 40 FPO signed MoU with seed farmers in 12 districts for procurement of seeds, and 40 varieties of Ragi landraces and 3 varieties of Ragi HYV seeds are planned for seed multiplication.

Budget Allocation under Odisha Millet Mission:

- Budget Allocation: Under OMM an amount of Rs361.84 Crore has been allocated and approved for the financial year 2022-23 and for the next 5 years i.e, from 2022-23 to 2026-27, Rs.2808.39 Crore has been approved for extension and expansion of the mission.
- Govt. of Odisha observing the International Year of Millets 2023, in-state through campaigns, media events, and collaborations for demonstrating its leadership in the millet promotion ecosystem through workshops, mega-events, and many more activities planned.

Plan of Odisha Millet Mission from 2022-23 to 2026-27:

- Increase in consumption of at least 25% to the baseline.
- Conservation and promotion of millet landraces in the state.
- Promote at least 500 post-harvest and processing enterprises with WSHGs/ FPOs
- Promote at least 500 millet-based value addition enterprises units with WSHGs/ FPOs
- To cover 500 to 2000 Ha per block under improved agronomic practices.
- To cover 4000 households in each program block through program interventions

- Promote 142 FPOs in 5 years. Promote custom hiring centers, and community seed centers in 142 blocks through FPOs/WSHGs
- Millet procurement from farmers through DBT in MSP
- Inclusion of millets in the Public Distribution System(PDS).
- Inclusion of millets in ICDS, MDM, Welfare hostels, and other Supplementary Nutrition Programmes in the State.
- Facilitating the millet markets and exports of millet-based products from Odisha through FPOs.

Learnings from Odisha Millet Mission:

1. Consult multiple stakeholders during the design phase. Focus on what worked in the field.
2. Actively onboarding multiple partners during implementation.
3. Community Organizations (WSHGs/FPOs) should be the backbone of the implementation.
4. Consumption centricity with a focus on local circular economies should inform agriculture interventions.
5. Situate project design in the cultural realities of field areas.
6. Willingness to modify/change scheme design as per field feedback.

Karnataka Organic Farming Policy:

In 2017, Karnataka launched a new Organic Farming Policy to enable the next level of development in organic farming and millet promotion. It was launched for incorporating new objectives and strategies and giving more focus to marketing. The policy emphasized on backward integration and forward linkages suiting the current dynamic market situation and consumer preferences. It was to popularize organic produce and millet as 'Super foods'.

Objectives:

The policy aimed to achieve the following objectives for the overall growth of the organic sector as well as the promotion of millets in the State with an ultimate goal of achieving sustainability in agriculture, providing safe and nutritious food for consumers, and ensuring remunerative prices to the farmers.

- To maximize the production and productivity of organics and millet.
- To enable farmers to mitigate and adapt to climate change and drought situations effectively.
- To maximize crop and farm diversification thereby enhancing protection against crop losses due to adverse weather conditions.
- To increase farmers' income by facilitating value addition to organic produce and millets thereby reducing post-harvest losses and other wastages.
- To create and strengthen local institutions for effective service delivery and sharing of knowledge and skills.
- To bring in more transparency in the production, handling, and marketing of organic produce and to safeguard the consumer interest.

In this initiative, minor millet-growing farmers were incentivized with Rs.10, 000 per hectare.

Financial assistance was provided for Millet processing machinery up to Rs.10 lakhs (50% subsidy). It has benefitted farmers with market linkages alongside providing value chain linkages between producers and consumers.

Maharashtra Millet Mission:

The Department of Agriculture, Government of Maharashtra started Value Chain Development of Millets through their SMART Project (State of Maharashtra Agribusiness and Rural Transformation). The main objective of the SMART Project is to support the development of inclusive and competitive agriculture value chains, focusing on smallholder farmers and agri-entrepreneurs in Maharashtra.

The project target cost is about Rs.21,000 crore, where the International Bank for Reconstruction and Development(IBRD) loan is Rs.1470 crore, share of the Government of Maharashtra is Rs.560 crore and the private sector CSR contribution is Rs.70 crore.

Under SMART Project, the sanctioned Detail Project Reports (DPRs) for Millet value chain development for Farmer Producer Company are as under:

Sr.No	Name of FPC	District	Sanctioned Project Cost Rs-Lakhs
1	Vinayak Farmer Producer Company	Kolhapur	149.63
2	Kumbhi Kasari Farmer Producer Company	Kolhapur	201.99
3	Chandgadh Farm Fresh FPC	Kolhapur	143.95
4	Sujag Farmer Producer Company	Solapur	40.48
5	Gensiddha Farmer Producer Company	Solapur	52.37
6	Ganesh CMRC	Solapur	72.75
7	Navi Disha CLF-MSRLM	Solapur	53.58
8	Manbhumi FPC	Solapur	145.27
9	Vincharana Farmer Producer Company	Ahmadnagar	129.70
10	Nirmiti Mahila Udyog	Ahmadnagar	42.56
11	Aaisaheb Agro FPC	Ahmadnagar	115.91
12	Rui Farmers Producer Company	Satara	156.38
13	Unnati CMRC	Dhule	20.65
		Total	1325.22 lakhs

For Kumbhi Kasari Farmer Producer Company, Kolhapur Rs.201.99 lakhs has been sanctioned for different components like Infrastructure and Storage of 250 MT, Cleaning grading unit of 2TPH, Pulveriser, Laddu making machine, Noodles making machine, Biscuit making machine, Flour testing machine, packaging machine and for Sundry.

In the proposed value chain of millet, they have focused on consumption, retailing, aggregation, primary, and secondary processing, marketing, production of millet, and input production involving different stakeholders. Institutions were connected for capacity building and assessment of sub-projects submitted by the Farmer Producer Organizations (FPOs).

Chhattisgarh Millet Mission:

Keeping in view of nutritional quality and health benefits of millets "State Millet Mission 2020" was launched by the Government of Chhattisgarh in the year 2021 with an aim to increase farmers' income by enhancing the acreage, production, and productivity of millets as well as enabling market arrangements for produce and processed product and to remove malnutrition by promoting domestic use of millets.

In 2021-22 "The State Millet Mission " is being jointly implemented by the Department of Agriculture, Forest and Environment with the convergence of various schemes to increase crop procurement and processing. Next year onwards millets product will be included in Public Distribution System by the Department of Food, Civil Supply, and Consumer Protection and will be used as a part of meals in the Hostel / School on a regular the basis by Department of School Education and Child and Women Welfare. The target for the next five years is to increase the total cultivated area from 83.73 thousand hectares to 186.40 thousand hectares and to boost productivity from 550 kg/ha to 1200 kg /ha of millets in Chhattisgarh.

Forest Development Corporation, Government of Chhattisgarh now started to purchase Ragi (*Finger Millet*) and Kutki (*Little Millet*) at Minimum Support Price as declared by the State Government. A total of 14 districts of the state are collaborating with the Indian Institute of Millets Research, Hyderabad for training on improved millet cultivation practices, food processing, and value addition.

The State Government will establish one Big Food Processing unit for Millets in each district for processing, value addition, and marketing. Secondly, a small processing unit in Gouthan (8 to 10 Gouthan as a Spoke) under RIPA as a processing and selling point will be developed. In addition to these, **Chhattisgarh e-Mart** will be set up to ensure delivery of millet produce and its processed products to the public/consumer.

The nodal department of "State Millet Mission 2020" is the Department of Agriculture and Farmers Welfare and Biotechnology. The Working Committee under the Chairmanship of the Chief Secretary at the State level and the Millet Mission Committee under the Chairmanship of the District Collector the at district level have been constituted for proper execution, supervision, monitoring, and review of the work done by block as well clusters.

Presently, in coordination with IGKV, SHG, and FPO various value-added processed products of millets such as Ragi flour, Ragi multigrain floor, Ragi Malt, Ragi Biscuit, Kodo, and Kutki as raw grain are now available in the market.

Millets crops are being popularized among farmers day by day as well as many consumers are getting satisfaction from the use of millets products which leads to rise in the number of millets product users.

Andhra Pradesh Millet Mission:

The Andhra Pradesh State government implemented a comprehensive project for the revival of millet cultivation by tribals in the north Coastal Andhra and parts of Rayalaseema. The programme intends to develop tribal, and rainfed areas into MILLETS-HUBS that can potentially supply millets to meet increasing demand.

The objective is to promote millet food tradition across all levels and help people drive home the message of the long-term benefits of including power-packed millets in the diet.

This project aims to increase productivity, household consumption, value-addition, marketing support, setting up processing units, and establishing seed production centers. In addition to that, a pilot inclusion of millet recipes for pregnant and lactating mothers was introduced with recommended nutrition standards. It mainly focused on the addition of millet food in the Supplementary Nutrition Programme (SNP) like YSR Sampoorna Poshana Yojana.

Telangana Millet Mission:

Millets were introduced into Anganwadi centers in Telangana to revive the consumption of millets and enhance the nutritional content of the hot-cooked meals served to children under ICDS. It was mainly for the children aged between 3 and 6 years, their mothers, and community members.

Millet Food festivals were organized to finalize the menu and build consensus around their inclusion in ICDS. The energy and nutritive values of the millet recipes were calculated to meet the standards. Millet Festivals were conducted to spread awareness about the benefits of millets and encourage communities to make millets a part of their diet. Feedback on the millet recipes was collected from the mothers, children, Anganwadi workers, and members of the community.

PART - VI
POINTS TO CONSIDER BEFORE STARTING MILLET STARTUPS

One

CHALLENGES IN MILLETS SECTOR AND HOW TO OVERCOME

In today's context, the millet sector has been facing a lot of challenges pertaining to the production of millets, processing, and value addition, marketing, and consumption. The challenges can be mitigated by taking extra efforts in solving the problems faced in the value chain of millets. The challenges are not only faced in India but also throughout the world. Let us understand what are the challenges faced in the millet sector.

Challenges in Millet Production:

1. **Low productivity of millets:**
   When we compare the productivity of millets with other crops like wheat, rice, and maize, it is very low. As you know millets are grown in marginal land with low fertility and most of them are rainfed which results in low productivity. Apart from these, there are many constraints in millet production. During my project work on millets, I could find the major constraints are weeds and most of the farmers cultivate millets in a traditional way. They simply broadcast the seeds on the onset of monsoon and harvest the crop after 75-90 days.

The yield gap of millets can be minimized if a proper package of practices is followed. It is found that for the farmers who practiced good practices like the System of Millet Intensification (SMI) in Finger Millet, the yield has doubled as compared to the traditional methods.

When millet farmers were asked about the factors that were to be followed to increase the yield of millets, the foremost response was sowing/transplanting on time, followed by weeding on time, proper nutrient management, and using improved varieties.

2. **Area under Millet is Declining:**

   It has been found that the area under millet is declining dramatically in India. If we compare the area under millets during the 1960s to the present scenario, it has reduced by more than 50%.

   If the fallow and wastelands are bought under millet cultivation, then the production can increase to much extent. Along with this, the millet farmers need to be incentivized to encourage them to grow millets.

3. **Resistance to Pests and Diseases:**

   As you know millets are hardy crops and very less infestation happens due to pests and diseases. But some pests and diseases often cause significant loss in major millets like Sorghum, Pearl Millet, and Finger Millet.

   If more cultivars with significant resistance to pests and diseases are made available to the farmers, this problem could be solved.

   I have marked a Finger Millet cultivar, ML-365 which is resistant to neck blast and is highly accepted by the farmers due to its yield and also fodder.

4. **Millet Seed Production:**

   Even today farmers are facing problems in getting quality millet seeds. Although there are no issues in Sorghum and Pearl Millet as private players have entered into this segment and made it available to the farmers in India.

There are opportunities to bring quality seeds of minor millets and this can be done by establishing seed hubs for breeding and producing seeds. This seed production needs to be demand-driven and all the stakeholders need to join hands together to improve the seed value chain.

There are many traditional millet varieties that are performing well in the farmer's field and these varieties need to be bought in the seed chain through Farmer Producers Organization. This intervention will help the farmers to get the right quality seeds and that too in time.

Challenges in Millet Processing:

The millet processing machines available in India have a low recovery of 70-80% of grains and this becomes a challenge for the millet processors. Due to less efficiency, the output has more un-hulled and broken grains. Dehulling efficiency of millets is affected by the impeller speed. As you know millet grains differ in size, shape, and husk content, so it becomes difficult to handle. Depending upon one dehuller for dehusking all types of millets is not suitable rather it requires two types of dehuller. As Kodo and Barnyard Millet contain multiple seed coats, it requires a double-stage dehuller to remove the husk.

Separation of the husk of millets and its collection is quite difficult as it causes spillage all over the processing unit and often gets mixed with the final product. Even many millet processors are facing difficulty in handling and disposing of the husk of the millets. If the husk of millets could be used in making value-added products, then the issue could be solved.

Millets being 100% gluten-free, it becomes very difficult to make some products with all total millet ingredients.

Still, more research and development are needed for enhancing the availability of nutrients and decrease the anti-nutritional contents.
Still, progress is continuing on improving the shelf life of processed millet grains. In today's scenario, the shelf life of millets is enhanced to 4-6 months. But to cater to the international market and exports from India, the shelf life of millets will be enhanced to a minimum of 12 months.

To overcome all the challenges in the millet sector, there is a need for constant efforts from all the stakeholders and institutions toward mainstreaming millet. It is not only addressing the challenges discussed above but also building forward and backward linkages by creating a better millet ecosystem. No doubt, the Government has taken a lot of initiatives in this last decade to bring millets to the plate of all and has taken vital steps to promote millets in India and also abroad.

Two

UNDERSTANDING END USER'S NEEDS AND BUILDING INNOVATIVE PRODUCTS

Over the decades, there has been a shift in preferences of foods by people and moreover, people have developed an inclination towards tastier food over healthier ones. So, it's time to develop innovative products with respect to the needs of the consumers. In this present context, understanding the end users and building innovative millet products is the need of the hour.

1. Innovative Millet Products:

How to improve the quality of the Millet Products?

- Varieties with specific end uses: India is a storehouse of valuable genetic variability. The nutrient content changes as the varieties differ. While developing a millet product the variety of millet needs to be taken into consideration. Suppose you are selecting Sorghum as the main ingredient for making pasta. Every variety of Sorghum is not suitable for making pasta. There are some specific varieties of Sorghum in which the pasta quality increases and you can get a better millet product every time. The Sorghum varieties are CSV-15, CSV-20, SPV-1253, SPV-1383 and SPV -1808.

I do remember, when we were conducting a Participatory Varietal Trial (PVT) on Finger Millet varieties in Odisha, I was astonished to see that the farmer prefers different varieties for different purposes in Finger Millet. One variety for selling in the market and the other one for their own consumption. The Finger Millet variety which is kept for his family's consumption is good in taste.

So, going specific to a millet variety we can develop good millet products.

- Sprouting and Fermentation: Sprouting of millet increases the bioavailability of nutrients in the body. As per the scientific study, the sprouting process showed more influence on the antioxidants and anti-nutritive factors. A comparative analysis of millets suggested that 24 hours of soaking and 24 hours of germination were found to be best for producing nutritionally enriched millet products. Tannin content decreases with an increase in germination. The phytase activity was found to be more when it is subjected to prolonged soaking and germination.

- Quality enhancement by blending and combining with other grains or pulses: For better retention of nutrients, phytochemicals, essential fatty acids, antioxidants, etc., you can go for freeze drying.

Freeze drying is a process in which a completely frozen sample is placed under a vacuum in order to remove water or other solvents from the sample. When millets are blended properly with other cereals and pulses, it results in better development attributes for the development of a wide range of millet niche products.

- Catering to functional foods: Millets can fit into the functional food category. You can put specific claims in your product and can have a complete advantage and in this way, you can provide health benefits to the consumers.

- Reduced anti-nutritional components from the millet products.
- Quality of proteins/other beneficial metabolites towards health benefits.

2. Taste drives the buying decision:

Taste is the most important factor for consumers to like and buy a product. According to a survey conducted by the International Food Information Council Foundation in 2020, 88% of people stated taste as their primary reason for buying a product.
So, taste should be the key focus during millet product development. It is also observed; people say that millet doesn't taste good. The perception of the people regarding millet needs to be changed and it can only be done by bringing innovative tasty millet products.

There are many factors when a consumer decides to buy a product for the first time. Maybe the beautiful packaging appeals to them, the labeling of the product, the price of the product or they are interested in trying innovative products. But repeating buying only happens if they like the taste of the product.

Repeat purchasing by the consumers creates loyalty which is essential for the product's success. If you do not have a repeat purchase you don't have a business.

It has to be noted that health awareness about millet alone will not be enough to influence people to consume millet, rather focusing on developing tasty and delicious recipes or products will help.

3. Brand Communication:

Brand communication is a broad term that involves activities such as advertising, reviews, and social media to communicate with consumers. It takes place every time a potential customer interacts with a particular brand. It is important for millet startups to spend time developing communication strategies because it is essential for building a brand.

4. Affordability:

When it comes to affordability people are looking for the best millet product they can buy at the best price available. It is essential to always keep this in mind while developing millet products. Apart from affordability, you must give product value to the consumers. In the context of Indian consumers who work hard to earn ten or hundred rupees, you are expecting to pay for the millet product that you have developed. So, you must always take the responsibility to provide double the value of the product to the consumers with the right quality and solve the problem he or she was looking for in your millet product.

REFERENCES:

1. Rajeswari N, Priyadharshini V. P. Evaluation of Nutritional and Nutraceutical Content of Polished and Unpolished Barnyard Millet - An Analytical Study. Curr Res Nutr Food Sci 2021; 9(3).doi : http://dx.doi.org/10.12944/CRNFSJ.9.3.31
2. www.milletadvisor.com - Millet Advisor
3. https://www.nin.res.in/ - National Institute of Nutrition, Hyderabad
4. https://milletsodisha.com
5. https://www.researchgate.net/publication/303662897_Foxtail_Millet_-_Nutritional_importance_and_cultivation_aspects
6. https://www.grandviewresearch.com/industry-analysis/gluten-free-products-market
7. https://www.thebetterindia.com/266427/miracle-millets-diabetes-indian-food-recipes-weight-loss-woman-entrepreneur/
8. http://organics-millets.in/assets/pdf/organic_millets_2017_eng.pdf
9. https://telanganatoday.com/hyderabad-based-millet-bank-empowering-women-farmers
10. https://www.millets.res.in/technologies/Technologies_of_millet_value_added_products.pdf
11. Impact of soaking, sprouting on antioxidant and anti-nutritional factors in millet grains G. Bhuvaneshwari1 , A. Nirmalakumari2 , S. Kalaiselvi1*

12. https://yourstory.com/2020/11/turning-point-soullfull-millet-breakfast-cereal-brand/amp
13. http://bwwellbeingworld.businessworld.in/article/In-Conversation-With-Prashant-Parameswaran-MD-CEO-Tata-Consumer-Soulfull/07-09-2021-403527/
14. https://timesofindia.indiatimes.com/life-style/health-fitness/diet/60-per-cent-of-indians-suffer-from-milk-intolerance-and-many-dont-even-realise-it/photostory/75807121.cms
15. https://provegincubator.com/alt-foods-the-startup-developing-plant-based-milk-from-grains-and-sprouted-millets
16. https://restaurant.indianretailer.com/article/restaurants-create-healthy-menu-with-millets.12168
17. https://www.thehindu.com/life-and-style/food/visakhapatnams-millet-idli-that-impressed-the-vice-president/article37703154.ece
18. https://www.usnews.com/news/news/articles/2022-07-01/india-bans-some-single-use-plastic-as-part-of-broader-plan
19. https://www.taste-institute.com/en/resources/blog/importance-of-taste-in-product-development
20. https://www.indiablooms.com/life-details/FD/6492/rise-in-millet-based-snacks-to-finding-cultural-roots-through-food-are-some-of-the-likely-trends-in-2022-says-report.html
21. https://theecopreneur.in/2021/10/14/machine-for-millets-try-a-small-millet-portable-impact-huller-smf-v2-developed-by-saravanan-from-dhan-foundation/
22. E-Commerce for Entrepreneurs - Dr.Sudeshna Chakraborty, Priyanka Tyagi
23. Millets: Strengthening Value Chains for Enhancing Nutritional Benefits and Increasing Farmers' Incomes - Food and Agriculture Organization of the United Nations, Ministry of

Agriculture and Farmers' Welfare, Government of India.
24. International Year of Millets (IYOM)-2023, National Conference on Kharif Campaign, Ministry of Agriculture and Farmers' Welfare, Government of India.
25. https://pib.gov.in/PressReleasePage - India begins exports of organic millets grown in Himalayas to Denmark
26. https://www.newindianexpress.com/cities/hyderabad/2022/aug/02/apollo-hospitals-sets-up-kitchen-to-provide-millet-based-diet-2483282.html
27. https://www.thehindu.com/life-and-style/food/visakhapatnams-millet-idli-that-impressed-the-vice-president/article37703154.ece
28. https://www.livemint.com/companies/start-ups/troo-good-raises-rs-55-crore-in-series-a-funding-from-oaks-asset-management-11636523489886.html
29. https://www.business-standard.com/article/companies/tata-consumer-products-to-continue-focus-on-acquisitions-122032600010_1
30. https://www.smartfood.org/
31. https://www.businesstoday.in/magazine/features/story/millet-cultivation-rising-in-india-oats-like-vs-wheat-rice-50472-2015-05-05
32. https://ediblepro.com/
33. https://tcrconnectingagriculture.com/2020/10/millet-processing-machine/
34. http://www.dhan.org/
35. https://www.traveldine.com/natasha-gandhis-house-of-millets-is-high-on-flavour/
36. https://inc42.com/buzz/kids-snackmaker-slurrp-farm-raises-7-mn-funding-from-icd-fireside-ventures

37. https://inc42.com/buzz/bollywood-actress-anushka-sharma-invests-in-d2c-snack-brand-slurrp-farm/
38. https://www.thebetterindia.com/221241/pune-woman-entrepreneur-organic-millet-baby-food-homemade-india-buy-online-ang136/
39. https://www.nutrihubiimr.com/white-paper
40. https://apeda.gov.in/apedawebsite/
41. https://www.dgft.gov.in
42. https://tradestat.commerce.gov.in
43. https://www.thebetterindia.com/262432/buy-earth-poorna-ragi-laddus-healthy-snacks-pune-online/
44. https://telanganatoday.com/hyderabad-based-millet-bank-empowering-women-farmers
45. https://yourstory.com/smbstory/24-mantra-organic-food-fmcg-farmers-hyderabad-business-entrepreneur
46. https://indianexpress.com/profile/author/shalini-rajani/
47. https://millets.res.in/pdf/success_stories/Compendium_Success_story_30-09-21_for_web.pdf

About the Author

Hello! **I am TAPAS CHANDRA ROY**

A Certified Farm Advisor on Millets with distinction and have been recognized by the National Institute of Agricultural Extension Management (MANAGE) and Indian Institute of Millets Research (IIMR), Hyderabad.

A cadet of Sainik School, Bhubaneswar, an agriculture graduate from Odisha University of Agriculture and Technology, and an MBA (Agri-Business Management) from Vaikunth Mehta National Institute of Co-operative Management (VAMNICOM), Pune. Currently working as Block Agriculture Officer-cum-Deputy Project Director, ATMA in the Department of Agriculture and Farmers' Empowerment, Government of Odisha, and serving the farming community.

I am promoting Millets from Farm to Plate so that the goodness of Millet reaches many people. On a mission to take the millets to millions. I am looking after the implementation of the Odisha Millet Mission at the ground level and helping farmers from sowing to harvesting by imparting training and providing Advisory Services. In addition to that, I am helping entrepreneurs, Self

Help Groups, and Farmer Producer Organizations in the millet journey.

I have a passion to develop delicious and innovative millet recipes and have been awarded at the National Level. I was the first winner for making Millet Rasgulla and runner-up in the Special Millet Biryani Millet Recipe Contest conducted by the Indian Institute of Millets Research, Hyderabad.

I am a Youtuber(> 16,000 subscribers) and a Blogger (www.milletadvisor.com) (8,000-10,000 visitors per month) on Millets. Created a Youtube Channel - TCR Connecting Agriculture in which I am promoting millets by covering Millet Technologies, Processing, Millet Farming, Recipes, and many more and helping and guiding millet entrepreneurs in their journey.

On these digital platforms, I am taking the initiative to share knowledge, skills, learnings, and all about millets so that awareness is created in this digital world and my advice and recommendations may help farmers, consumers, entrepreneurs, and all other stakeholders in their decision-making.

I have done a Project Work on ""Utilization of Finger Millet in Nutritional Security"" in Koraput, Odisha in 2020 where I worked with farmers, NGOs, and the workers under ICDS Programme and assessed the triggering mechanism for incorporation of Finger Millet in the regular diet of men, women, and children.

I have contributed to the ""White Paper on Millets"" as a Task Force Committee Member submitted to Niti Aayog, Government of India. I have shared my experience and knowledge in Agriculture Production, Climate, Post-Harvest Processing and Policy Status, and Prescription on Millets.

I was Invited as a Speaker in Krushi Odisha held at Bhubaneswar and delivered my talk on the theme ""Millets for Climate Resilient Agriculture and Nutrition Security"" in 2021.

I was appointed as a Rapporteur in the Nutri-Cereals Multi-Stakeholders Mega Convention held at Hyderabad in Sep-2021.

I was a Guest Speaker at 15 Days International Online Training on """Advances in Agri- preneurship and skill development for reshaping the future of Indian Agriculture""" and delivered my talk on """Role of Millets and Business Opportunities for Entrepreneurs""" conducted by Just Agriculture Magazine in 2021.

Delivered my experience in the Workshop on Assessment and Documentation of Good Practices, Lessons learned and Preparation of Policy Briefs for Millets Mainstreaming conducted by World Food Programme (WFP) and IPE Global at Krushi Bhawan, Bhubaneswar in 2021.

My expertise may be utilized in academic, research and extension activities related to Millets for better advisory services.

Represented Odisha Millet Mission in different states and Union territories like Tamil Nadu, Rajasthan, Chandigarh, Delhi, and Telangana.

I was presented with a Certificate of Appreciation for my exemplary commitment towards Scheme implementation and farmer welfare under Dakshyata from the Department of Agriculture and Farmers' Empowerment, Government of Odisha in 2020.

Finally, I have a passion for Millets.

If you like my book, please join me by subscribing to my Newsletter on Millets at www.milletadvisor.com and connect with me on LinkedIn. And let all your friends and relatives know about this book. I also request you support the book by writing reviews or by sending a testimonial to tapas@milletadvisor.com.

www.ingramcontent.com/pod-product-compliance
Lightning Source LLC
LaVergne TN
LVHW012054160826
845678LV00014B/2829

* 9 7 9 8 3 6 1 5 0 1 9 6 0 *